Parenting for Faith

By Andrew Mullins:

Parenting for Character (also published by Scepter)

Parenting for Faith

Parenting for Faith

Why Love for the Sacraments Matters Most

ANDREW MULLINS

Scepter

Published by Scepter Publishers, Inc.
info@scepterpublishers.org
www.scepterpublishers.org
800-322-8773
New York

Text Design: PerfecType, Nashville, TN
Cover Design: Studio Red Design
Cover Art: Alamy.com

Library of Congress Control Number: 2021947548
ISBN (pbk): 9781594174483
ISBN (eBook): 9781594174490

Printed in the United States of America

For Tinashe and Oscar,
men in the making.

Contents

Introduction

Yours is a supernatural task requiring supernatural resources.

–Jonathan Doyle[1]

For Catholic parents, parenting includes two big tasks: First, caring for our child's *natural life* by feeding and clothing them, keeping them safe, fostering their growth in character, and teaching them the truths we know naturally through reason and experience; and second, nurturing their *supernatural life*, the relationship they have with God through prayer, worship, and the sacraments. Nurturing their supernatural life means

---

1. This is a recurring theme of the talks and podcasts of Jonathan Doyle who addresses tens of thousands of teachers and parents each year. www.jonathandoyle.co/episodes.

teaching them to live joyfully, in a relationship of love with God our Father, with Jesus, and with the Holy Spirit, and to extend that love to others in a spirit of self-less service.

This book aims to help you, the father and mother, to build up your children's supernatural life in the most effective way possible, through the sacraments. We want our children to have the very best the Catholic Church can give, namely, the help of the sacraments throughout their lives. The seven sacraments—baptism, confirmation, the Eucharist, penance, the anointing of the sick, holy orders and matrimony—lead us through our spiritual journey.[2] If you want to maximize the likelihood that the Catholic faith will flourish in your children and bear the fruit of a happy and virtuous life, then you should grow it with the grace of the sacraments.

My goal is that this book assists you in teaching your child about the new life brought to us through the sacraments. Nobody is better placed to do this than you, as your child's parent. It is your privilege to teach your child

---

2. Thomas Aquinas, *Summa Theologica*, trans. Fathers of the English Dominican Province (New York: Benziger Brothers, 1911-1925), III.65.1.

to love God with all their heart, soul, and strength, and in the process your life will be immeasurably enriched.

The quality of your parenting counts. Clear-headed, positive parenting is precisely aimed at empowering a young person with the virtues they will need to love wisely with all their being. When virtues are guided by the realities of faith, they are supernatural virtues by which we live out our Christian vocation.

There is no gap between sensible parenting and raising children to love God and their Catholic faith. When homes are not effective, the faith is rarely passed on. "The best predictor of what the religious and spiritual lives of youth will look like is what the religious and spiritual lives of their parents look like."[3] But your parental example of piety is not enough—if we want children to develop a deep commitment to religion, we need to be emotionally supportive, and talk to them personally and frequently about our own faith.[4]

---

3. Christian Smith and Melinda Lundquist Denton, *Soul Searching: The Religious and Spiritual Lives of American Teenagers* (New York: Oxford University Press, 2005), p. 261.

4. Gary D. Bouma, G., *Australian Soul: Religion and Spirituality in the Twenty-First Century* (Port Melbourne, Victoria: Cambridge University Press, 2006); Mark Regnerus, Christian Smith, and Brad Smith, "Social Context in the Development of Adolescent

Throughout this book, my experiences as a boys' school headmaster in Sydney, Australia, with friends, families, parents, and students are used to illustrate a number of points about the importance of the sacraments. Most of the people I refer to will remain anonymous, but their comments illustrate the challenges of living up to the demands of faith in a well-developed society. These events led me to see firsthand how powerful were the effects of the sacraments on both children and adults at all stages of life. I pass them on in the hope that they will be reflected in your stories and in the events of your life.

Religiosity," *Applied Developmental Science* 8, no. 1 (January 2004), pp. 27–38; Kath Engebretson, "'God's Got Your Back': Teenage Boys Talk About God," *International Journal of Children's Spirituality* 11, no. 3 (2006), pp. 329–345; Kenda Creasy Dean, *Almost Christian: What the Faith of Our Teenagers Is Telling the American Church* (New York: Oxford University Press, 2010); R. Keating, "Towards a Holistic Approach to Spirituality," *Journal of Religious Education*, 48, no. 4 (2000), pp. 16–21; Judith A. Cashmore and Jacqueline J. Goodnow, "Agreement Between Generations: A Two-Process Approach," *Child Development* 56, no. 2 (April 1985), pp. 493–501.

CHAPTER 1

Why Do Sacraments Matter So Much?

By praying with their children, by reading the word of God with them and by introducing them deeply through Christian initiation into the Body of Christ . . . they become fully parents, in that they are begetters not only of bodily life, but also of the life that through the Spirit's renewal flows from the Cross and Resurrection of Christ.

—St John Paul II,
Familiaris Consortio, 39

A young couple were disagreeing about what type of high school was best for their son. The non-Catholic father wanted to move him into an academically challenging but secular school. The mother wanted to keep him in a Catholic school that emphasized their faith, where a school chapel provided the opportunity to attend Mass regularly and to receive the sacrament of reconciliation. They were asking my thoughts at a school function where senior students were serving the refreshments. I noticed a boy standing nearby: Nick, who was one of our best students and whose sister was attending the kind of school the father preferred. I knew where his loyalties lay, so I brought him into the conversation: "Nick, what would you say about the advantage of leaving here to attend a more exclusively academic school?" He replied, "I know I would do as well there as here. But here, I have learned about the sacraments. I have been given something for life."

I was not expecting such an answer. "Something for life." Not just for life here on earth, but for eternal life.

The gifts of life and of supernatural life are the greatest gifts God gives us. And it is through the sacraments that we enter and sustain supernatural life: "through them divine life is bestowed upon us."[1] Sacraments communicate God's love and life to us. They are indispensable for all Catholics. The sacraments are the greatest sign of God's love for us. St. Paul urges us, "Let all that you do be done in love" (1 Cor 16:14). Love is our ticket to heaven.

Study after study demonstrates that the greatest factor in helping faith take root in a child's life is the religious practice of the parents.[2] And the greatest single factor in whether Catholic children become practicing adult Catholics is that they have grasped the vital importance

---

1. *Catechism of the Catholic Church* (New York: Image Doubleday edition, 1997), 224.

2. For example: Beau Abar, Kermit L. Carter, and Adam Winsler, "The Effects of Maternal Parenting Style and Religious Commitment on Self-Regulation, Academic Achievement, and Risk Behavior Among African-American Parochial College Students," *Journal of Adolescence* 32, no. 2 (April 2009), pp. 259–273; Randal D. Day, et al., "Family Processes and Adolescent Religiosity and Religious Practice: View From the NLSY97," *Marriage & Family Review* 45, nos. 2–3 (2009), pp. 289–309; Douglas L. Flor and Nancy Flanagan Knapp, "Transmission and Transaction: Predicting Adolescents' Internalization of Parental Religious Values," *Journal of Family Psychology* 15, no. 4, December 2001, p. 627; Scott M. Myers, "An interactive Model of Religiosity Inheritance: The Importance of Family Context," *American Sociological Review* 61, no. 5 (October 1996), pp. 858–866.

of sacraments. Why? Because in the seven sacraments, through apparently ordinary actions, God bestows extraordinary graces. These graces have the power to transform our lives so that we step through the challenges of life with uncommon strength, peace, and joy. The sacraments are the greatest gifts of love from Jesus to his Church, and a parent is God's instrument to pass on these great manifestations of his grace and love.

The sacraments are our source of strength, yet so many drift away from them. One Catholic mother, herself at Mass every day, says, "I have ten grown children. I love every one of them, and they are good to me. But not one of them goes to Mass." Across the Western world, church attendance had dropped dramatically. Barely 6% of French Christians are now at church weekly.[3] In Ireland congregations have been dropping every year over the last decade by over 3% yearly from the 40% attending weekly in 2010.[4] Church attendance for Australian

---

3. "Frequency with which Christians go to church or temple in France in 2020." Statista website: https://www.statista.com/statistics/1238643/church-temple-attendance-among-christians-france/.

4. "Irish Census (2016)," Faith Survey website: https://faithsurvey.co.uk/irish-census.html; Patsy McGarry, "Mass attendance in Dublin to drop by one-third by 2030," *The Irish Times*, January 21,

Catholics is at an all-time low: in 1947, some 63 percent attended weekly Mass, but by 2011, the figure was 10 percent and falling.[5] One father tells me his son is the only child in his Catholic secondary school class who attends Sunday Mass. In one Catholic primary school I know, a teacher tells me that two families out of one hundred and fifty are attending Sunday Mass. In another, it's five out of five hundred families. One bishop has described this drop in practice as "the most alarming reality"[6] that we face in the education of children.

Why is this happening, and how did it happen? Why does God allow families to be so apparently ineffective? It helps to look at history, particularly biblical history, where it happened before. When Jesus taught that the greatest commandment is to love God with all one's heart, soul, and strength (see Lk 10:27), he was drawing on an Old Testament tenet: "You shall love the Lord your God with

2016, https://www.irishtimes.com/news/social-affairs/religion-and
-beliefs/mass-attendance-in-dublin-to-drop-by-one-third-by-2030
-1.2504351.

5. Peter Wilkinson, "Who goes to Mass in Australia in the 21st Century?" Catholica, September 6, 2013, https://www.catholica.com
.au/gc4/pw/005_pw_print.php.

6. Jarrett, Bishop Geoffrey. "Catholic Church and her schools face a 'wake-up call'." *AD 2000 Magazine*, (February 2006): 7.

all your heart, and with all your soul, and with all your might" (Dt 6:5). In that Jewish scripture, the next passage specifies, "You shall teach [these words] diligently to your children, and shall talk of them when you sit in your house, and when you walk by the way, and when you lie down, and when you rise" (Dt 6:7).

Why these reminders? The Chosen People were given an extraordinary gift: possession of a fertile, wealthy land, with cities, houses, farms, and produce of all kinds. It was a premodern consumer society where they could easily live and prosper—and also forget who provided it. Thus Moses warns them further: "Take heed lest you forget the Lord, who brought you out of the land of Egypt, out of the house of bondage" (Dt 6: 12).

We can't say that we were not warned. He is talking to us. Affluence can all too easily lead us to forget the Lord. The Hebrews entered the land of milk and honey that God himself was preparing for them. Milk is a symbol for sufficiency in all our needs, and honey stands for all the sweet add-ons. God warned them not to become distracted by the good things and so forget that God must remain at the center of our heart and soul and mind.

Fast forward. No culture has been more advanced, and spoiled, than our own. In our age, we have all the milk we want—everything we need—and a big jar of honey—so many sweet things. We live in the most comfortable countries in the most affluent age of civilization, and as a consequence, we forget God.[7] Out of the one hundred billion persons ever to have lived, we are the most fortunate. But do we remember our Lord's words of warning about how hard it is for a rich man to enter the kingdom of heaven?

A good parent tries to sow desires in a child's heart: desires for what is good, true, and beautiful. Yearn for God and teach this to your children. It is Jesus himself who tells the rich young man, "No one is good but God alone" (Mk 10:18). He describes himself as the way to follow God, since that's why he, as God, became a man: to model for us how to follow God. Yet how many dead-end paths we choose instead. We allow our hearts to yearn for the wrong things. We are surrounded by bright and shiny attractions and distractions, and if something captures our eye, it is but a short step to wanting to possess it. We

---

7. United Nations Development Programme, "Human Development Report 2016," (New York, NY: One United Nations Plaza, 2016), http://hdr.undp.org/sites/default/files/2016_human _development_report.pdf.

must learn to manage our attention: the more we look at something, the more likely we are to want to possess it.

Have you noticed that the ninth and tenth commandments warn us not against actions but against wrong desires? Where our eyes go, our thoughts go; where our thoughts go, our desires go. Let's raise children to manage their "FOMO," their "fear of missing out." In God we have everything we need: "The Lord is my shepherd, I shall not want" (Ps 23:1).

Stealing the Young

The milk and honey trap is all the more dangerous because of peer attitudes. In every age parents have had a battle on their hands to be the decisive influence on their children's values.

Nazi Germany is a case in point. Pope Pius XI had to remind German Catholic parents that no matter what the government was teaching, they were responsible for teaching the faith to their children. Pius XI started his letter of March 14, 1937, with the words, "With deep anxiety." The Pope stressed the duty of parents to oversee the education of their children, to claim the space:

[N]one can free you from the responsibility God has placed on you over your children. None of your oppressors, who pretend to relieve you of your duties can answer for you to the eternal Judge, when he will ask: "Where are those I confided to you?" May every one of you be able to answer: "Of them whom thou hast given me, I have not lost any one" (Jn 18:9).[8]

The message was and is simple and urgent. Parents have a God-given mission that is a privilege and duty. Nobody else has the right to set the moral and spiritual agenda for your child.

Fast forward to the present. Every age has had its challenges and while we may no longer have to worry about the fourteen-year-old going to camp with the Hitler Youth, parents should know what other "milk and honey" is being fed into their minds. To prevent that, what culture are you creating at home?

---

8. Pius XI, Encyclical Letter *Mit Brennender Sorge* (March 14, 1937), 39. Vatican website: https://www.vatican.va/content/pius-xi/en/encyclicals/documents/hf_p-xi_enc_14031937_mit-brennender-sorge.html.

Create a Domestic Church

The urgent duty to form their own child's head and heart falls on parents. Both doctrine and piety are needed; lessons in truth and in love. Diligent parents of every age have nurtured the faith and practice of their children explicitly and by example.

Look what St. Louis IX, king of France, wrote to his son, the future King Philip III.

> Dear Son, the first thing I advise is that you fix your whole heart upon God, and love Him with all your strength, for without this no one can be saved or be of any worth. . . . If our Lord send you any adversity, whether illness or other . . . you should receive it in good patience and be thankful for it, for you ought to believe that He will cause everything to turn out for your good. . . . If our Lord send you any prosperity, either health of body or other thing you ought to thank Him humbly for it.[9]

---

9. "St. Louis' letter of advice to advice his eldest son," as quoted in Medieval Sourcebook, January 26, 1996, https://sourcebooks.fordham .edu/source/stlouis1.asp.

And adversity did come to Philip. His father died suddenly and Philip found himself crowned king, yet almost immediately, Philip's pregnant wife died, thrown from her horse. Perhaps he reread the timely advice of his saintly father. History records Philip as the pious and courageous son of his father.

Five hundred years later, Catherine of Aragon wrote to her daughter referring to her dealings with her father, Henry VIII, a less than ideal role model:

> Answer with few words, obeying the King, your father, in everything, save only that you will not offend God and lose your own soul. . . . I will send you two books in Latin; the one shall be *De Vita Christi* [On the Life of Christ] with a declaration of the Gospels, and the other the Epistles of St. Jerome that he did write to Paul and Eustochium, and in them I trust you shall see good things.[10]

We know, too, that St. Thomas More's daily custom was, "besides his private prayers, to say with his children

---

10. Marilee Hanson, "Letter of Katharine of Aragon to her daughter, Princess Mary April 1534," as quoted in English History, February 24, 2015, https://englishhistory.net/tudor/letter-katharine -aragon-daughter-princess-mary-april-1534/.

the Seven Psalms, litany and suffrages following, and, before he went to bed, with his wife children and household, to go to his chapel and there upon his knees ordinarily to say certain psalms and collects with them."[11] He would spend every Friday in his chapel, recollected from morning till evening. And it wasn't as if he didn't have enough to do: he was Chancellor of the Realm!

Do we talk this way, and give this type of example, to our children? St. John Paul II wrote a letter to families in which he stressed these duties:

> One area in which the family has an irreplaceable role is that of *religious education,* which enables the family to grow as a "domestic church". . . . Even when they entrust these responsibilities [to others] their educational presence ought to continue to be *constant and active.*[12]

---

11. William Roper, *The Life of Sir Thomas More* (c. 1556), ed. Gerard B. Wegemer and Stephen W. Smith (2003), 15, https://www.thomasmorestudies.org/wp-content/uploads/2020/09/Roper.pdf.

12. John Paul II, Letter to Families *Gratissimam Sane* (February 2, 1994), 16. Vatican website: https://www.vatican.va/content/john-paul-ii/en/letters/1994/documents/hf_jp-ii_let_02021994_families.html.

Think about composing a family mission statement. What would you include? What daily customs are present in your home that integrate your faith into family life?

Raw Material for Holiness

The moral strength of your child's character depends on the four cardinal virtues: the four habitual dispositions human nature requires to manage our desire for pleasure, to overcome our fears, to measure our actions by their impact on others, to set the right goals for ourselves, and, as a parent, for our young children.

Through temperance and fortitude a child is equipped with habitual dispositions in their emotional life so they can think clearly. Through prudence their planning is effective, and through justice they habitually take others into account. "The door to happiness opens outward," Kierkegaard concluded. We must learn to focus on others if we wish to be happy.

- Fortitude and temperance are habits of emotional self-management, without which a child's thinking is easily highjacked. Without fortitude, our fears overcome us, and we are unable to put up with pain even when there is an important reason. Without temperance, we are dragged off course by a thousand and one distractions. Pleasure becomes our master.

- Prudence or sound judgment plays the guiding role so that we act with clarity of conscience, the habitual readiness to live in reality, and the ability to set effective goals for ourselves. It encompasses sincerity and humility.

- Justice, also sometimes called respect and responsibility, is another great prerequisite. It is the habitual recognition of our duties to others—first of all to God but also to family members, friends, and all others. Justice is the source of generosity, piety, and religious and filial duty, of obedience to one's parents, and ultimately of happiness.

These cardinal virtues each need to be present in each of our actions. Keep in mind that virtue is an all-or-nothing affair. Without the emotional management of temperance and fortitude there is no possibility of rational choices, and when justice and charity are lacking, our choices are self-serving.

Aristotle explained that virtues require both training of our responses to pleasure and pain, and education, so as to give ourselves good reasons for action. Both are essential. He insisted on the connection between repeated behaviors and responses, and the type of person we are becoming. He insisted that men, by "slack lives . . . become unjust or self-indulgent" and therefore that parents should inculcate positive repeated behaviors.[13] He insisted on the need for parents to inculcate positive repeated behaviors.

The capacity to manage our emotional lives is at the very heart of character and of effective action. A person enriched by, but not dominated by, emotion is capable of facing the truth and setting goals accordingly, of entering relationships with others based on loving dedication and not simply on self-interest. As human beings our lives are greatly enriched by emotions that enable us to empathize deeply with others, increase understanding of situations, and empower us to throw ourselves into great projects.

The more your child interiorly struggles to be virtuous, the more easily they connect with others, the better

---

13. *Nicomachean Ethics*, trans. W.D. Ross (London: Oxford UP, 1959), 1114a3-8.

their choices in relationships, life, and faith. And the happier they are. Parents and teachers provide the early training in these four strengths.

From the Church children receive baptism, bringing the theological virtues into play: prudence is enriched by faith and hope, and justice is enriched by charity.

Natural strengths of character, such as courage and generosity, can be put at the service of our faith, becoming what we call supernatural virtues. Human virtues are transformed into qualities that give glory to the Father: we courageously live out our faith despite criticism; we generously give our time to prayer and to those in need, out of love of God.

St. Paul tells us to "have this mind among yourselves, which was in Christ Jesus" (Phil 2:5). To have the mind of Christ, we must build on the human virtues. If we wish to think like Jesus, the prerequisites are self-mastery of our emotional life by the virtues of temperance and fortitude, complete readiness to direct our life towards God and others by the virtue of justice, and the capacity to set faith-filled, prudent goals for our action. In this way all a child's choices can be actions carried out with a personal love of God, an exercise of supernatural virtue.

Children do not form such character automatically. It is the task of parents to give close guidance, encouragement, and calm correction. We train them to love what is good (to pay attention to the Blessed Sacrament, to honor Mary with a flower), to overcome their fear of discomfort to do whatever is good (to tidy up after play, to say sorry if they offend). We teach them right and wrong, in the light of our faith, so they can judge their own actions with a clear and correct conscience, acting in gratitude to God's great love for us.

Our example is essential. Let us do some systematic soul searching to see where we have work to do on our characters if we are to love God with all our heart, soul, mind, and strength, and our neighbor as ourselves. By virtues we unite ourselves with those we love. Let us examine how well we are exhibiting in our own lives the four cardinal virtues and the three theological, infused virtues of faith, hope, and charity.

Fix Your Face

Time and again I have met parents deeply regretful when they give their children the example of anger. We have an intuition that our emotional example is at the very heart of the essential life lessons we pass on to children. It is as if there is a small voice inside, warning us of dire consequences if we let such behavior become entrenched.

A rather volatile friend felt himself starting to boil over, yet he was determined not to get angry again at his daughter, only seven years old. Tonight however, she had again pressed him too far. He went into the laundry and shut the door and composed himself. Finally he came back into the family room. Immediately his daughter jumped behind her mother and, looking warily at her father, said, "Daddy's got the face." Joe thought he had fixed his face, but it was there for all the world to see.

Kids know much more than we think, adept as they are at reading the *habitual* emotional response of their parents. A little girl drew a picture of her parents one night at home, and it gave Dad something substantial to think about: Mom wore a smile, but Dad had a frown.

From the first weeks, a baby is focused on her mother's face, and soon will be imitating smiles. A child's capacity to imitate easily is a marvelous learning mechanism. We now know that these neural mechanisms for imitation are not simply focused on learning discrete skills like poking out our tongue in response to a parent doing the same. Rather, psychologists have linked imitation of facial expression to the development of a child's emotional life.[14] Autistic children are known to have less capacity for imitation learning, and so they find it harder to develop the emotional responses of their peers.[15]

When we give positive and cheerful facial examples, we teach children to stay cheerful and positive. We must also teach children to make good choices about where they seek happiness. When we model the peace and joy which derive from sacraments, prayer, and a living faith, we lay the foundations for the child's own mature trust in God.

Our emotional response is at the core of our motivation. We are attracted to what we delight in. We avoid what we fear or find difficult. If not well-managed, emotions are liabilities. We can be paralyzed by fears and anxieties, or become slaves to our appetites for pleasure, power, admiration, or possessions. Emotions can distort our view of reality, but through the development of the virtues of temperance and fortitude we learn to manage

14. Susan Hurley, "The Shared Circuits Model (SCM): How Control, Mirroring, and Simulation Can Enable Imitation, Deliberation, and Mindreading," *Behavioral and Brain Sciences* 31, no. 1 (2008), pp. 1–22.

15. Giacomo Rizzolatti, Maddalena Fabbri-Destro, and Luigi Cattaneo, "Mirror Neurons and their Clinical Relevance," *Nature Clinical Practice Neurology*, 5, no. 1 (January 2009), pp. 24–34.

our emotional lives, and in this way we can *choose* rather than *run on impulse*. Because they are habits, we reach the point that we are drawn to what is good for us.

Happiness and sadness are key motivators in life; kids see our happiness and they learn that birthdays, or jokes around the dinner table, or a thousand other things are good things. They see our sadness at something authentically wrong, and they further calibrate their moral world. If they see us angry with them, they will be fearful at first, and blame themselves. The assumption of a small child's world is that a parent's anger is justified. Older children may see through this and become resentful of parental anger. But the bottom line is that when parents lack self-control they send confusing signals to their children.[16]

Remember, all you say and do leaves a trace. Do you teach that there is more joy in people than in things, in faith than human outlook? Service to others in the family must bring more joy than computer game distractions. Let us model optimism; joy in what is good, true, and beautiful; and joy above all in faith and in family. It can help to work as a team, giving each other feedback, to

16. This was the inescapable message of a survey of children's communication with parents which we conducted at Redfield College, Sydney, where I served as headmaster.

create a positive culture in the home by the emotional tone of your feedback.

Let us respond with desires for holiness, with efforts to love with deeds more than good intentions, and above all with our joy. A faith that does not bring us joy is catastrophically unconvincing. Children will conclude that such a life cannot be worth the effort. And for this reason, families without infectious joy and generous service to each other are in danger of failing. Even the atheist philosopher Nietzsche understood this when he said that Christians would be far more convincing if they were more joyful.[17]

Why the Sacraments Are Important

It had been a tough afternoon. I had flown to the funeral of Paul, one of my oldest friends. We had known each other since the start of high school. After his diagnosis with motor neuron disease he told me his goal was to come much closer to Jesus Christ. I found inspirational the equanimity with which he carried himself as the

---

17. Friedrich Wilhelm Nietzsche, *Human, all too human: A book for free spirits*, (Edinburgh: T.N. Foulis, 1910), 6.

illness took its toll. He continued his work at a veterinary research station as long as he could. After the funeral, his son, voted captain of his Catholic school, dropped me off at the airport. We spoke about his classmates. I asked him if they were attending church. Loyally he spoke up for them, "Not many of my friends go to church. They are spiritual but not religious."

Is it possible to be spiritual but not religious?

In the broad sense we are all spiritual: we have non-material powers of knowing and loving. Dogs and cats can't do that. But can we be in union with Jesus Christ in our souls if we don't seek the help he offers us to stay close—help that is given primarily in the sacraments? Jesus can bring close to him anyone he wishes, but *we* don't make the rules in this game.

Is it possible to opt out of the Church and still stay spiritual? Pope Benedict points out that it is through the *community* of the Church that we receive the sacraments.[18] Without the institutional Church we are high and dry, bereft of spiritual resources.

---

18. Benedict XVI, Encyclical Letter *Spe Salvi* (November 30, 2007), 10. Vatican website: https://www.vatican.va/content/benedict-xvi/en/encyclicals/documents/hf_ben-xvi_enc_20071130_spe-salvi.html.

We need the Church because God's life in our souls comes to us first via the sacraments of the Church. Trying to get ourselves to heaven without sacraments would be as foolish as wanting to play international soccer without ever joining a club, as wanting to be an actuary without knowing mathematics. We would have forgotten that we are embodied creatures and that we need structures, not as an end in themselves, but for training and support.

Pope Francis has reminded us that the "sacraments, celebrated in the Church's liturgy," pass on the "fullness" of "her living Tradition, . . . the new light born of an encounter with the true God, a light which touches us at the core of our being and engages our minds, wills and emotions, opening us to relationships lived in communion."[19] Without the Church, we lose this.

Each of the seven sacraments has its origin in the New Testament. Each was instituted by Christ himself. The *Catechism of the Catholic Church* puts it this way: "Through the Church's sacraments, Christ communicates his Holy

---

19. Francis, Encyclical Letter *Lumen Fidei* (June 29, 2013), 40. Vatican website: https://www.vatican.va/content/francesco/en/encyclicals/documents/papa-francesco_20130629_enciclica-lumen-fidei.html.

and sanctifying Spirit to the members of his Body" (739). They are the firehoses of grace. Alone we can do nothing. Everything else is a dripping tap.

Do you recall the moment in the long Good Friday liturgy when we listen to St. John's Passion? Our Lord's side is pierced by the lance, and immediately, in the eyewitness testimony, blood and then water gush out. The Catholic Church has always seen this outpouring as the graces mankind receives because of our Lord's loving sacrifice, distributed to us principally through the sacraments.

New Testament origin of each sacrament	
Baptism	Mt 28:19, Jn 3:5, Acts 2:38, Rom 6:3-4.
Confirmation	Acts 19:3-6, Heb 6:2.
Holy Eucharist	Mt 26:26-29, Lk 24:35, Acts 2:42, 1 Cor 11:24-27.
Penance and Reconciliation	Mt 16:19, Jn 20:21-23.
Anointing of the Sick	Jas 5:14-15.
Holy Orders	Acts 6:3-6, Acts 13:2-3, 1 Tm 4:14, 1 Tm 5:22.
Marriage	Mt 19:10-11, Eph 5:31-32.

The water also reminds us that Jesus gave everything. Just as the Jews were forbidden meat that still contained any blood, so too the sacrificed Jesus has given all his blood. He is truly the Paschal Lamb.

In this short book we are looking at ways to raise children with a deep personal love of God, to raise them in grace. The starting point is that *we* must be convinced that without the sacraments we would be spiritually starving; we must lead by example and show the joy they give us. From their earliest years, your children need to witness your reliance on the sacraments.

First, this must happen by our example. We must pray like *we* mean it, with the conviction that prayer is heard.

Next, Dad's role is crucial. A young couple were going through a very difficult time. They had four small children. He was changing jobs, she had just been diagnosed with breast cancer, and they were going to counselling. They were arguing incessantly. Then Dad's decision to give spiritual leadership in the home made all the difference:

> I realized that I had to stop leaving the spiritual leadership in the home to my wife. I was passive and too apathetic. I started to bring the kids

together for our family prayers every night. I ask my daughter to light a candle at the picture of Our Lady in the hallway, and each of us leads a prayer. That has changed everything!

Third, the more personal the better. Ours is a religion in which God has revealed himself. We are inestimably privileged to have received this message. God has not only spoken to us, he has walked among us and is still with us in the Eucharist and in our souls. Blaise Pascal wrote that ours is the "God of Abraham, God of Isaac, God of Jacob."[20] Our God is not the God of philosophers and sages who could only propose some benevolent creator.

In prayer we meet God the Father, God the Son, and God the Holy Spirit in a very personal way. We meet Mary and the saints. We meet the guardian angels. In prayer, and nowhere else. The gift of faith hinges on our belief, and our belief hinges on accepting the testimony of a person we can trust. So, if we do not meet Jesus in prayer, if we do not respond in prayer to Jesus' presence in the Blessed Sacrament, to Mary's motherly care for us, we will find our faith growing weaker.

---

20. Romano Guardini, *Pascal For Our Time* (New York: Herder, 1966), pp. 33-44

Fourth, routines help greatly. We are creatures of habit. So many adults remember the morning offering and the night prayers they learned from their mothers' lips. Pope Francis draws particular focus to family grace before and after meals. And many parents find that children grow quickly to love the Rosary.

Ed, struggling with some family issues, speaks of how he was trying to put more attention into helping his children grow in their faith. He explained the Rosary to his ten-year-old daughter and urged her to say it well. A few days later he realized his daughter was awake at six in the morning saying the complete Rosary to herself. Another parent, Anne, heard talk coming from the boys' room after lights out. She opened the door, saying "Dom, be quiet. Why are you talking so much?" "I'm saying the Rosary," he replied.

In the chapters ahead you will find . . .

- For each sacrament, there is an inset box with a simply worded explanation of what the Church teaches about this sacrament.
- Each chapter focuses on one sacrament, with seven subsections, each with a practical parenting suggestion.

- At the end of each chapter there are points for reflection about one's parenting.
- For the first four sacraments—baptism, confirmation, Eucharist, and reconciliation—the emphasis is on leading your child into the supernatural world of our faith, teaching them most of all by your joy, and your personal example of prayer and dependence on the grace of the sacraments.
- For the sacrament of the sick, the focus is on teaching children to bear the greatest challenges of life with faith and love for God's will.
- In the consideration of holy orders the focus is on leading children to appreciate Providence and discover the path to which God is calling them and therefore in which they will be most happy.
- Finally, for the sacrament of Marriage, the focus is on passing on deep formation in the beauty of human love.

CHAPTER 2

Baptism

You are those who transmit the faith, the transmitters; you have a duty to hand on the faith to these children. It is the most beautiful inheritance you will leave to them: the faith! Only this. Today, take this thought home with you. We must be transmitters of the faith. Think about this, always think about how to hand on the faith to your children.

–Pope Francis

Homily at Administration

of the Sacrament of Baptism,

Sistine Chapel, January 12, 2014.

When John the Baptist is asked, "Are you he who is to come, or shall we look for another?" (Mt 11:3), he answers that his baptism is only with water but that the Christ "will baptize you with the Holy Spirit and with fire" (Mt 3:11). This description of the Messiah highlights Jesus' greatest gift to us, the life of the Spirit. Eternal life. And this gift of "new life," of God's life in our soul, comes at the moment of baptism. For this reason, baptism, this inheritance of eternal life, is the greatest gift that a parent can give a child.

Parental Privilege and Responsibility

Michael, a young father of seven, tells the extraordinary story of how he came to be baptized.

> When I was born, my father was not going to church, but he knocked on the parish door and said, "Father, I want you to put some water on my son's head."
>
> "No," replied the priest. "Not until I see you here every Sunday for the next year."
>
> If that priest had not said "No," I would not be a Catholic today. You can't pass on to your children

what you do not have yourself. I am so grateful to that priest.

How well that priest understood that parental example is almost everything when it comes to education of children.

Let's consider our example. What a privilege to become fully parents in faith! But we must treasure this invitation.

In the local parish there is a day seminar required of parents who are asking for the baptism of a child. One presenter described these gatherings: "Often parents just want to get it over with. It's hard to hit a chord and it's hard to generate enthusiasm. Sometimes there are complaints, 'Why do we have to sit through this? This is for my child, not for me.'" Weak on faith, we can easily reduce parenting to feeding, sheltering, and nurturing with affection.

Baptism is unique among the sacraments. That we normally receive it before we are aware of what we are doing says a great deal about God's love for us. Just as a baby receives care and nourishment before asking for it, so the Church offers the same spiritual sustenance. Think of the first battles little children have to wage against themselves—obeying even when tired, owning up to a mistake, saying sorry to a little sister—and how much it helps if grace is already strengthening the soul during these first experiences of free choices.

Jesus Gave us Baptism

Jesus tells us that baptism is necessary for salvation: "He who believes and is baptized will be saved; but he who does not believe will be condemned" (Mk 16:16). He says to Nicodemus, "Unless one is born of water and the Spirit, he cannot enter the kingdom of God" (Jn 3:5).

Of course God can give salvation to whomsoever he wishes, but the normal pathway to salvation that Jesus wishes to give us requires baptism and a life characterized by love of God.

Jesus gave us the example of seeking baptism. He came to John for baptism not because he needed it, but because he wanted to show its importance. He commanded his followers, "Make disciples of all nations, baptizing them in the name of the Father and of the Son and of the Holy Spirit, teaching them to observe all that I have commanded you" (Mt 28:19–20), and the disciples understood this clearly: on the day of Pentecost alone they baptized three thousand (Acts 2:47).

Like baptism, all the great events of the New Testament are prophesied in the Old. Baptism is foreshadowed by the Great Flood, the crossing of the Red Sea, and the rite of circumcision: new life flourished after the flood; salvation came by means of the crossing; and the seemingly human action of circumcision entitled the Jews to God's favor and to possession of the Promised Land.

How Soon Do We Baptize?

The Church recommends infant Baptism should not be delayed but given during the first days of life, as soon as the care of the baby and health of the mother permit. However, so important is the role of the parents, without the permission and support of the parents a child should not be baptized unless in danger of death.

What happens when we receive baptism? St. Paul tells us we become "a new creation" (2 Cor 5:17). Our soul participates in the divine life of the Trinity, and we are made Christlike—sons of the Father, and sharers in the priesthood of Christ. How could it be that when our team wins we are more delighted than we are on the day of a child's baptism? Do we really understand that there is no greater good for a human being than to be in the grace of God?

Baptism is our passport to a spiritual country where the Father opens his palace to us, where Jesus is our travel guide and mentor, and where living for others is the only currency. Infused with faith and love, we become capable of acting with love of God. Our faith is the greatest gift we could receive, so let us strive to treasure it accordingly, teaching children to value it by our own manifest joy and gratitude. Baptism is the bridge to the transcendent life of faith. St. Leo the Great wrote, "This gift exceeds all gifts: that God should call man son, and man should name God *Father*."[1]

The Baptismal Liturgy

1. The candidate, or the parents of an infant, expresses the desire to receive the sacrament and take on the duties that baptism involves.
2. We listen to readings from Scripture that highlight the baptismal mystery.
3. Homily.
4. We pray for the intercession of the saints.
5. There is a prayer of exorcism and an anointing with oil, signifying divine protection.
6. The baptismal water is blessed.
7. An act of faith and a renunciation of sin are made.
8. The water is poured on the head of the candidate three times (or the candidate is immersed), while the words "I baptize you in the name of the Father and of the Son and of the Holy Spirit" are pronounced.

---

1. Leo the Great, Sermo 26. Website: https://www.newadvent .org/fathers/360326.htm.

9. Various actions follow the baptism. The head of the candidate is anointed, signifying the gift of the Holy Spirit and the sharing in the common priesthood of the faithful. A white garment signifies baptismal innocence. A candle lit from the Pascal candle, representing Christ, reminds us that we are now children of the light. The priest touches the ears and mouth of the newly baptized to stress the importance of listening to and proclaiming the Word of God. We recite the Our Father, reminding us that we are now children of God.

Baptism Changes Everything

Sometimes we glimpse better the greatness of baptism from the testimonies of adults who have asked for baptism. I will not forget the return to school of Takuya, who had just lost his mother to cancer. He brought us a letter from his father.

> To the Teachers, Parents and Students of Redfield College,
>
> Thank you for your special prayers since Keiko first became so ill. My wife, Keiko Cecilia Yoshida, was taken to God on February 17 at 41 years of age.

Together with a Catholic priest, my three children and I were at her side in the hospital in Tokyo at that time. A Mass and Funeral Service were held on February 19.

When Keiko was in hospital in Sydney in January, the Doctor, with my consent, told her that she had cancer. Thereafter she told us that she would become mad,

1. If she had not converted (she was baptized Catholic after marriage),
2. If she did not have three children, and
3. If, after being told she was seriously ill with cancer, she could not have had an Australian priest to console her.

We talked in Keiko's room at the Hospital in Tokyo of how lucky she was because so many people prayed for her recovery, but that if God was to call her to heaven, she would give protection to these friends and family from there. This was our final discussion together in this world.

It is of great consolation to me that Keiko told her mother how happy she had been to be married with me. Thank you once again for your thoughts and prayers, as I believe you are very supportive of my family. I would like to offer you my family photograph taken at home last December when we were all together.

> Yours sincerely,
> Naoya, Natsuki, Takuya and Haruka

Takuya went on to become school captain and a top student. He returned to Japan, played rugby for Tokyo University, met his future wife, and is now a very proud father.

What gave Keiko her strength to face the trial of the illness and her separation from family? She saw her Catholic faith as the critical difference. She married into one of the old Catholic families of Japan—forgotten heroes who passed on the faith for ten generations, without the help of priests. We sense the strength she derived from her baptism and from the help of the priest aiding her with the sacrament of the sick, of reconciliation, and of the Eucharist.

Baptism gives us a new identity; we become a child of God. At baptism we hear the words, "You have become a new creation clothed with . . . Christian dignity. Receive the light of Christ. Keep the flame of faith alive in your heart."[2]

A parent's role is not just to ensure a newborn is baptized without undue delay but also to model what it means to love God, to be a child of the Father, to model how we should respond to the greatest privilege that a human being can receive. The task of parents is to second the great grace that has been received. The baptismal liturgy urges the parents: "Make it your constant care to raise your child in the faith."[3]

We Are Never Alone

Baptism is not a symbolic but peripheral moment in our lives. Adopted as children of God, we look at all reality in a new light. The task of each of us is to live our own baptismal calling in all its richness, to model what it means to be a child of God—just as Keiko and Naoya in their different ways were able to do.

---

2. Catholic Rite of Baptism for One Child. Available at: https://www.ibreviary.com/m2/preghiere.php?tipo=Rito&id=103.
3. Catholic Rite of Baptism for One Child.

The Effects of Baptism

Baptism brings marvellous effects. We receive supernatural life, which is the grace that Adam and Eve lost by their original sin and so were unable to pass on to us. We receive the indwelling of the Blessed Trinity in our souls, so we become "temples of the Holy Spirit" (1 Cor 6:19) and are made Christlike, "children of God" (Rom 8:16), and we become members of his Mystical Body, the Church.

Baptism also forgives the personal sins and punishment due to those sins that we are conscious of having committed before we are baptized.

Baptism also brings duties. With privilege comes duty: to seek holiness and to be a faithful follower of Christ, sharing in his task of bring the world and all people to God.

James Mawdsley drew international attention to atrocities in Burma. Three times arrested, he described his prison ordeals in *The Heart Must Break: The Fight for Democracy and Truth in Burma*.[4] He suffered beatings, a broken nose, solitary confinement, intimidation,

---

4. James Mawdsley, *The Heart Must Break: The Fight for Democracy and Truth in Burma* (London: Century, 2001).

and hunger. During his second imprisonment, which included torture, he returned to his Catholic faith. On his release he reflected on how his faith helped him when he was in jail.

> I was never in solitary confinement. God was there. He carried me like a shepherd with a lamb. I felt the Almighty wonder of his presence. I felt the love of Jesus; sweet enrapturing, exalting, devastating Love. My absolute weakness made way for his absolute strength. He granted the Grace of his Holy Spirit, for calm wisdom and impossible courage. Blessed, I was in a new reality. His Love, his Word, the eternal Peace. This is fact. Am I worried about returning? No way.[5]

He did return a third time and was sentenced to seventeen years in prison, but in the ensuing year caused so much grief to the junta, by way of sanctions and negative publicity, that they ejected him from the country a year later. Once back in England, he was interviewed by the popular TV host David Frost and ran for Parliament. He

---

5. James Mawdsley's personal and unpublished emails to family, reproduced with permission.

is now a Catholic priest. His experience of being accompanied has been repeated time and again in the lives of saints and martyrs, and of many folk whose stories never make the headlines. It is a promise to us all, by baptism.

Finding Our Father

The 2003 witness of Yekaterina Trenozvikova, a nineteen-year-old Kazakh university student, captures the discovery in baptism of the Fatherhood of God from her totally different perspective:

> Years ago I only prayed because I was afraid of being punished by God. Nevertheless I was already being punished, because I was far from Him. I didn't know much about God and the Holy Trinity at that time. My image of God was very vague—the Creator who gave life to people. That was all. . . . I never thought about God's Love, about all His precious gifts; I never thought that people could be close to Him.
>
> How did I become Catholic? A friend of my mother invited me to Holy Mass. At that time, the services were held in a small chapel, but I

was deeply impressed by the prayers and thoughts of God, reflecting in everyone's eyes. . . . Soon I understood that it was impossible to live far from God. One who lives in a dark dungeon must dream about seeing light. . . . Life without God is just existence; it is like a winter valley, without grass or flowers. Even if a small flower appears, it will be killed by severe winds—by sins, despair, disappointment, lack of faith. Could I live such a life, especially when I learned that there was a cure for it? So I decided that I must seek God and never go far away from Him again.

In the Church library I read books . . . about our Father, kind and merciful, who through confession can forgive your sins. So I converted because I felt that the Catholic Church could bring me to salvation and could be my Home. . . . Men and women can come to this source. . . . They have a chapel in their heart and they can hear God speak to them in a whisper. And, what I like most of all, they will never grow up, but their faith will grow from day to day.

. . . Some years ago I used to say, "Nobody cares for me. Nobody will lift a finger for me if I ask them." But now, looking at the altar, I think that there is someone who cares, someone who not only cares, but who gave his life for me. We young people are too much possessed by pessimism, pay too much attention to small problems. Still, they cannot be compared with the sufferings of Jesus, who died on the cross for us.[6]

Baptism must bring with it the discovery of the great goodness of God and his great care for us. God is our Father. He has brought us home into the heart of his divine family and bestowed on us "precious and very great promises" (2 Pt 1:4). We discover the great gift of divine filiation that comes with baptism: the capacity to see the greatness of God's love for us, and that he only has plans of great kindness for us.

So, even when there are difficulties and apparent tragedies, St. Paul teaches that God our Father is drawing out good for those who love him. St. John Paul writes bluntly, "Suffering is present in the world in order to

---

6. An edited version of this talk is to be found in Yekaterina Trenoznikova, "A Message Which Is Simple Yet Profound," in *Youth: Building the Future. Proceedings of "The Grandeur of Ordinary Life" Congress* (Rome: Edizione Universita della Sante Croce, 2003), pp. 45–48. We spoke together in a panel at this conference.

release love."[7] At every level this is true, both in experiencing the care of those around us and in the growth of our own love of God. Keiko, even in the midst of the challenge she faced, was able to respond with deep gratitude to God for her life.

Let us teach those in our care to make God the point of reference for their lives:

> Have no anxiety about anything, but in everything by prayer and supplication with thanksgiving let your requests be made known to God. And the peace of God, which passes all understanding, will keep your hearts and your minds in Christ Jesus. (Phil 4:6–7)

Our Lord is our brother who leads the way and shows us how to act. Jesus refers to the Father explicitly, some 110 times in the Gospel of St. Matthew alone, and continuously during his passion: "Father take this cup," "Father forgive them," "Father into your hands."

---

7. John Paul II, Apostolic Letter *Salvifici Doloris* (February 11, 1984), 30. Vatican website: https://www.vatican.va/content/john -paul-ii/en/apost_letters/1984/documents/hf_jp-ii_apl_11021984 _salvifici-doloris.html.

St. Paul explained that the Divine Spirit of Jesus within us, the Holy Spirit, leads us to address God as our Father:

> For all who are led by the Spirit of God are sons of God. For you did not receive the spirit of slavery to fall back into fear, but you have received the spirit of sonship. When we cry, "Abba! Father!" it is the Spirit himself bearing witness with our spirit that we are children of God, and if children, then heirs, heirs of God and fellow heirs with Christ, provided we suffer with him in order that we may also be glorified with him. (Rom 8:14–17)

Big Shoes to Fill

The most privileged moment of my teaching career came at the bedside of a colleague, Michael Douglas, a few days before his death.

Michael was a loyal friend. Trish, his wife, had phoned that afternoon to tell me that Michael had just moved to palliative care. "Come if you can," she said. When I arrived, Michael was lying in silence with glazed eyes, unable to acknowledge his wife, his daughter, or me.

After perhaps an hour like this, without a word, he abruptly sat up. He looked steadily at his daughter, who was also a teacher, and then at me, and said clearly, "Students must see Christ in their teachers." Then he sank back into the bed and lapsed into his previous state.

"Students must see Christ in their teachers." If this is true for teachers, of course it is doubly true for parents. Christ is our model, "the true and finished man of character."[8] Parents will be effective only when they strive to be Christlike. "Put on the Lord Jesus Christ," St. Paul urges us (Rom 13:14). Let us honor God our Father in all we do, and so strive to live for others, as Christ did: in other words, a life of prayer and service, drawing strength from the sacraments.

To copy Christ has been the goal of Christians of all ages. Mother Teresa wrote:

> Thoughtfulness is the beginning of great sanctity. If you learn this art of being thoughtful, you will become more and more Christ-like, for his heart

---

8. Pius XI, Encyclical *Divini Illius Magistri* (December 31, 1929), 96. Vatican website: https://www.vatican.va/content/pius-xi /en/encyclicals/documents/hf_p-xi_enc_31121929_divini-illius -magistri.html.

was meek and he always thought of others. Our vocation, to be beautiful, must be full of thought for others.[9]

It was the desire to imitate Christ that motivated Dr. David Livingstone too, in his explorations and missionary work. He wrote, "My great object was to be like Him—to imitate Him as far as He could be imitated. We have not the power of working miracles but we can do a little in the way of healing the sick and I sought a medical education in order that I might be life Him.[10]

Only One Sorrow Existed There . . .

The year was 1903. Jacques Maritain and Raïssa Oumansov, two nineteen-year-old philosophy students at the Sorbonne in Paris, were deeply in love. They sat talking on the banks of the Seine. They had not a shred of faith, and, profoundly discouraged by the apparent pointlessness of existence, they came to an agreement: should they

9. As quoted in Malcolm Muggeridge, *Something Beautiful for God: Mother Teresa of Calcutta* (New York: Harper & Row, 1971), p. 51.

10. As quoted in William Garden Blaikie, *The Personal Life of David Livingstone* (London: John Murray, 1888), p. 185.

not discover a purpose in life within six months, they would take their lives. Raïssa reflected, "I would have accepted a sad life, but not one that was absurd."[11]

Within weeks, they met Léon Bloy, an impoverished Catholic author who was to change their lives. When they visited him, they wanted the treasure they found in his home. Jacques later described their visits to Bloy's family:

> Once the threshold of this house was crossed, all values were dislocated as though by an invisible switch. One knew, or one guessed, that only one sorrow existed there—not to be a saint. And all the rest receded into the twilight.[12]

Soon after their marriage the Maritains were baptized, on June 11, 1906, in the Church of St. John the Evangelist in Montmartre. Friends thought Maritain had fallen into the hands of the Jesuits; they denounced Bloy as a fanatic. Another friend told Jacques he had committed intellectual suicide, while others accused him of betraying progress. They were wrong. Jacques Maritain

---

11. As quoted in Ralph McInerny, *The Very Rich Hours of Jacques Maritain: A Spiritual Life* (Notre Dame, IN: University of Notre Dame Press, 2003), p. 16.

12. As quoted in McInerny, p. 22.

became perhaps the greatest Catholic philosopher of the twentieth century. His books became reference texts for Vatican II and, more than any other philosopher, he was responsible for the rebirth of Thomism. All this came in spite of poverty, Raïssa's chronic ill health, the loss of their best friends in the First World War, and flight from France before the Second War.

Raïssa's own mystical writings are a treasury of spiritual gems. Among the insights given to her in prayer were the words, "You are always asking what you ought to do: the only thing is to love God and serve him with all your heart."[13]

Holiness is for all. The call to whole-hearted, whole-souled holiness is central to our faith. "Be perfect, as your heavenly father is perfect," Jesus urges in the Gospel of St. Matthew (5:48), and St. Paul also insists, "This is the will of God, your sanctification" (1 Thes 4:3). The Second Vatican Council teaches that all "are called to the fullness of the Christian life and to the perfection of charity."[14]

---

13. Raïssa Maritain, *Raïssa's Journal* (Albany, NY: Magi Books, 1974), p. 105.

14. Vatican II, Dogmatic Constitution on the Church *Lumen Gentium* (November 21, 1964), 40. Vatican website: https://www.vatican.va/archive/hist_councils/ii_vatican_council/documents/vat-ii_const_19641121_lumen-gentium_en.html.

This universal call to holiness has been described as the very "democratization of sainthood."[15] In the great encyclical reflecting on goals for the new millennium, St. John Paul presented this as the key focus for the Church, and more specifically for schools: "Catholic schools . . . are above all to be schools of holiness. They exist primarily to give saints to the world."[16]

Holiness must be practically packaged, and for this, St. Josemaría Escrivá, whom St. John Paul called "the saint of ordinary life,"[17] had a knack. He insisted on the need to be united with God in our daily work, to bring God into our family lives, and to plan our day with times for prayer and sacraments. Above all, holiness consists of

---

15. Janne Haaland Matlary, Speech "Work a Path to Holiness" (2002), p. 170. Josemaría Escrivá de Balaguer and Opus Dei Virtual Library, University of Navarre: file:///Users/raissa/Downloads/Work-a-Path-to-Holiness.pdf.

16. John Paul II, Speech "Address to Catholic Educators" (March 17, 2000), Sydney Stadium: Australia. As quoted in Jim Quillinan, "Linking Parishes, Schools and Families – a Call to Holiness through Life Long Learning," The Australasian Catholic Record 81 (October 2004), pp. 387-396. Website: https://search.informit.org/doi/abs/10.3316/ielapa.869512696701541.

17. John Paul II, Speech "Address of John Paul II in Praise of St. Josemaría Escrivá Founder Opus Dei" (October 7, 2002), 2. Vatican website: https://www.vatican.va/content/john-paul-ii/en/speeches/2002/october/documents/hf_jp-ii_spe_20021007_opus-dei.html.

love of God. He wrote, "Sanctity is not a matter of doing things that are more difficult each day, but rather of doing them each day with more love."[18]

This is a message that even small children can grasp—some sooner than others. "What do you want to be?" a dentist asked. The eight-year-old boy replied, "A millionaire." The next patient, a little girl the same age, answered equally without hesitation, "A saint."

Desires for holiness can be sown very early. It is a most sublime parental privilege (but also a duty) to raise children to be saints, and our commitment to this task tells us a great deal about how seriously we take the call to holiness.

The Only Path to Holiness

Holiness is a gift, but somehow that gift depends on our good desires and efforts. There is only one path to holiness: love. Scripture could not be clearer. The benchmark is, "Love one another as I have loved you" (Jn 15:12). In other words, we must learn to give our lives for others

---

18. St. Josemaría notes from his preaching, as quoted in Ernst Burkhart and Javier Lopez, *Ordinary Life and Holiness in the Teaching of St. Josemaría*, Volume II (New York: Scepter, 2020), p. 256.

as Jesus did. The worth of our lives depends on whether we die to ourselves: the grain of wheat that falls into the ground and dies yields a rich harvest. Parents, with the myriad of daily family demands on their generosity, have a head start in this. But we should remember that "it is more blessed to give than to receive" (Acts 20:35).

So when you look back, long after your child is an adult, how will you measure your parenting success? Human beings are fulfilled by living in the truth and loving wisely, so there are two critical questions.

- Have you passed on your most cherished values to your son or daughter?
- Have you raised your son or daughter to be successful in permanent relationships of love with God and with others?

These goals are interdependent. We fail to flourish if we are selfish. Pope Francis insists, "We are all called to be holy by living our lives with love and by bearing witness in everything we do, wherever we find ourselves."[19]

---

19. Francis, Apostolic Exhortation on the Call to Holiness in Today's World *Gaudete et Exsultate* (March 19, 2018), 14. Vatican website: https://www.vatican.va/content/francesco/en/apost _exhortations/documents/papa-francesco_esortazione-ap_20180319 _gaudete-et-exsultate.html.

We cannot build a spiritual life, nor raise children well, if we are egotistical. There is no room for pacts with impulsive behaviors, for complaining, for heads obsessed with our own plans. Such example will derail your child's capacity to think clearly, and so love wisely. For our children to be happy, we must strive daily to fix ourselves.

After Baptism

Model these convictions, attitudes, and actions, and talk about them to your child:

- Faith
- Gratitude
- Divine Filiation

Ages for principal focus on these goals: 0–7

Pray about these areas of example in your own life as a parent.

- Am I grateful for the privilege of raising a young person to love God? Does this gratitude make me joyful?
- Do I draw strength from God's life in my soul? Am I aware that God always accompanies my family?
- Are my worries entrusted to God my Father? And so do I have habitual peace of heart?

- Is Jesus Christ my model, so that I seek to think his thoughts and act as he would act?
- Am I determined to be holy?
- We fail to flourish when we focus on ourselves. Do I fight against selfishness in my life, in my marriage, and in my parenting?
- Do I nourish the great gift of faith through habits of prayer and frequent sacraments?

Education of head: Sow these convictions in your child.

- God is my Father and he only sends me what is good for me, even if it is difficult.
- I thank God every day and ask his help to be good.
- I say simple prayers every day.
- We visit Jesus in the Blessed Sacrament whenever we have the opportunity.
- I show my love for God and others by listening, serving, and obeying.
- We love God by always treating our family and friends well.

Education of heart: Education of a child's desires and feelings.

- Praying makes me happy.
- Knowing that God is my Father gives me a holy pride.
- Visiting Jesus in the Blessed Sacrament makes me happy.
- Helping my parents brings me joy.
- I love to obey and to help.
- I know how to say sorry and try again to be better.

CHAPTER 3

Confirmation

In our era, the road to holiness necessarily passes through the world of action.

—Dag Hammarskjöld

The great, first secretary general of the United Nations

Consider this incident: Gabrielle, eleven years of age, is completing a survey that her Catholic school catechist has given to the class at the start of a new year.

Mother: "Catholic. Not practicing."
Father: "Non Catholic. Didn't want to."

Brothers: "Michael. Non-Catholic."
Me: "Gabrielle. Catholic by my own choice."

Courageous and independent words: "By my own choice." By our choices we cooperate with the graces that the Holy Spirit sends us. We make choices, plans, and set goals which, with divine help, we will be able to carry out in our lives. We should take responsibility for our impulses and "not gratify the desires of the flesh" (Gal 5:16). We should also take care of our thoughts: "If there is anything worthy of praise, think about these things" (Phil 4:8). Lastly, we should control our actions: "If we live by the Spirit, let us also walk by the Spirit" (Gal 5:25). The Holy Spirit can only guide our lives when we freely and attentively seek out and listen to his inspirations in our soul.

By confirmation we are further initiated into our Catholic faith. This sacrament perfects our freedom and rationality, which are key characteristics of our humanity, whereby we share in "the image and likeness of God."[1] For this reason, confirmation is normally received after we reach the age of reason, empowering us to suffuse our love of God into each one of our actions and interactions.

---

1. *Catechism of the Catholic Church*, 1700.

The Rite of Confirmation

Confirmation is normally conferred once the candidate has the power of reason, about seven years of age. The candidate should be well instructed about the sacrament and its effects, receive it willingly, and have no unconfessed serious sin.

A bishop or his delegate celebrates the sacrament. First there is a renewal of baptismal promises and a profession of faith. Then the bishop extends his hands over those to be confirmed and the person is anointed on the forehead with chrism (a mixture of olive oil and balsam) as the words "Be sealed with the gift of the Holy Spirit" are spoken. The ceremony concludes with a sign of peace signifying communion with the bishop.

Confirmation strengthens us for the personal responsibility which must accompany free choices, whether we are young or old. Mature choices are the task of a mature Christian. The sacrament of confirmation equips us to make free and responsible choices in the light of faith, to be Christlike in our choices.

Through baptism and confirmation we are invited to infuse all we do with the theological virtues: believing the great truths that God has shared with us, trusting in his plans for our salvation, and imbuing all our actions with his own love.

The Seven Gifts

Let's look at another case. James was a very happy and popular ten-year-old student and marvelous soccer player. He was not Catholic. About one year after coming to a Catholic school, he asked to be baptized, but not because his friends were Catholic. When he was asked why, he said simply, "I want to be more like Jesus Christ." The school spoke to his parents, who willingly committed to support him in his newfound faith, and he started his preparation.

What does it mean to be more like Jesus Christ? Is it like saying "I want to be more like Roger Federer"? Very much so—it is to have the very qualities that you admire. If Jesus is the model of my personality rather than the model of my backhand, it means that I want to possess his virtues in their entirety, knowing that he is true man as well as true God and so has a human personality in full perfection. Confirmation gives us the power to do this. We receive the gift of the virtues of Jesus Christ, but in a form whereby we still must do our part.

Baptism infuses faith and charity into our virtuous actions, empowering us to act with love of God in all our deeds. Confirmation perfects supernatural virtue through what we call the seven gifts of the Holy Spirit: wisdom, understanding, counsel, fortitude, knowledge, piety, and fear of the Lord. These are supernatural virtues in their fullness, *as Jesus himself possesses them.* In possessing these supernatural virtues, we become truly Christlike. We know ourselves as sons and daughters of God our Father and recognize that our life's purpose is to give glory and thanks to the Father, loving God with our whole heart and soul and strength. We see the world as creation, as something that is good yet not an end in itself. The gifts prepare us to stand up bravely for our faith, to the point even of giving our lives, just as Jesus gave his life.

These gifts perfect the supernatural virtues, allowing us to act as Christ, in a divine way of acting.[2]

- Understanding applies faith to better grasp revealed truths.

---

2. *Summa* II–II.19.7. The *Summa* also states: "For the gifts of the Holy Ghost are the origin of the intellectual and moral virtues [. . .] while the theological virtues are the origin of the gifts . . . (II-II.19.9).

- Knowledge helps us to rightly judge created things in relation to their supernatural purpose to give glory to God, drawing on hope so that we can achieve the supernatural purpose of our own lives.
- Wisdom acts with charity, filing us with a boundless gratitude toward God and choosing God as the ultimate cause of all goodness.
- Counsel perfects prudence, giving us certainty about what is fitting to reach our ultimate end.
- Fortitude is the habit of overcoming all difficulties and obstacles to love of God.
- Piety perfects justice, granting us an habitual awareness of our adoption as children of God.
- Fear of the Lord perfects temperance, whereby we desire God above all, avoiding all distractions.

Lessons from Perfect Parents

What can parents today learn from the way Our Lady and St. Joseph raised our Lord? Our first reaction might be to say, "Parenting would be easy if all children were *that* good." But we should look more closely, to unravel the clues in the gospel.

Jesus Institutes Confirmation

During his public life, Jesus showed us his union with the Holy Spirit. He spoke in the synagogue at Nazareth and told us that he possessed the Spirit of God: "The Spirit of the Lord God is upon me because the Lord has anointed me to bring good tidings to the afflicted" (Is 61:1). We are told, so that we imitate him, that he was led "by the Spirit" into the desert (Lk 4:1). Twice the Holy Spirit in the form of a dove was seen to descend upon him.

At the Last Supper he promised that he would send the Holy Spirit to us, to remain with us forever as a friend and advocate, and indeed the Spirit did descend spectacularly on the apostles at Pentecost.

The Old Testament had already foreshadowed this coming of the Holy Spirit with the words of Joel: "Even upon the menservants and maidservants in those days, I will pour out my spirit" (Jl 2:29).

Effects of Confirmation

Confirmation brings a deepening of baptismal graces: offering us a deeper awareness that we are sons of the Father, uniting us more firmly to Jesus, perfecting our membership in the Church, and granting us the gifts of the Holy Spirit— wisdom, understanding, knowledge, counsel, fortitude, piety, and fear of the Lord. The gifts are the supernatural virtues, as possessed by Jesus himself. In exercising them we imitate him more perfectly. In addition, confirmation empowers us to profess and defend the faith in our words and deeds.

When Jesus was twelve, he was lost in Jerusalem for three days. The incident is related in the second chapter of St. Luke, and we reflect on it each time we say the Joyful Mysteries of the Rosary.

Mary was the perfect parent, and St. Joseph hangs second in the parenting hall of fame. If we study their actions, we learn what perfect parents do, and how they act in certain situations. Just because Jesus was perfect man doesn't mean that he didn't grow and acquire experience just as other children do. St. Luke tells us, "Jesus advanced in wisdom with the years, and in favor both with God and with men." He was true *child* as well as true *man*.

We can trace the personalities of Joseph and Mary that we see in Jesus. Think of his parables, with their unassuming profundity. No doubt his flair for storytelling came from Joseph or Mary. His sense of humor was no doubt like theirs, just as your own child laughs at the same things you do—consider his smiling irony after Philip is amazed that Jesus saw him under the fig tree (John 1:50). But most of all, he acquired from Joseph and Mary the strengths of his human character. From them he learned to do "all things well" (Mk 7:37). He learned virtues in a family life where love and respect for God and others were the underpinning of all else. In fact he would not have been a perfect child if he did not seek to learn all he could from his parents. The fact that Joseph was not his natural father does not diminish his role in the formation of our Lord's human character: an adopting parent leaves a profound and permanent mark on his adopted child.

Only after a full day's traveling away from the city do Mary and Joseph realize that the twelve-year-old Jesus is missing. They had thought he was with other relatives among the large group of pilgrims in which they were traveling. For three days they searched for him, retracing their steps, and finally come across him in the temple.

The detail of the words spoken between the child and his mother when they are reunited in the temple testifies to an eyewitness account of the event. Indeed, it is the common belief of Scripture scholars that Luke's source of information for much of his Gospel is none other than Our Lady herself. Furthermore, Luke tells us numerous times during his Gospel that Mary kept a detailed recollection of events in her heart and meditated on them.

Many thought-provoking parenting pointers lie just below the surface in this incident: the unity between Joseph and Mary, the importance of raising a child with physical and emotional self-sufficiency by the time adolescence is starting, their readiness to listen before judging, their readiness to correct affectionately, and their ability, when they did not understand his reasons, not to escalate the situation or to get cross. They trusted him and they were humble.

Let's focus on the questions that Mary, the perfect mother, asks: "Son, why have you treated us so? Behold, your father and I have been looking for you anxiously" (Lk 2:48). Her whole educational focus is to instill self-management based on self-knowledge and awareness of duties to others. And when her son's reply is beyond her understanding, she does not seek to have the last word. Mary is telling us that we have a duty to measure all we do by its impact on those around us. Parenting fails most gravely when a child has not been taught to treat God and others well.

Confirmation is most often conferred on a child of the age of Jesus in this story, or perhaps a year or two younger. Just when a child is learning to struggle to overcome impulsive behaviors by reflecting on his own actions and his duties of charity to others, the sacrament gives us actual graces to act in ways that honor God.

Putting Prayer in Our Schedule

On the north island of New Zealand is an inlet commanded by a majestic headland high above the ocean. This is Mount Maunganui. From its 760-foot summit, cargo ships heading toward the island look like toy boats. At all daylight hours, locals and tourists trek to the top. Some years ago I decided that I would hike to the summit to see the dawn. Once there I sat on a rock to gaze down over Tauranga, the town below. The next moment, a man accompanied by a teenage boy was standing behind me, and he said mischievously: "Excuse me, you're sitting on my prayer rock." We started talking. "Are you locals?" I asked. "Yes, I'm the Baptist pastor. My church is down there, and I come up here three mornings each week to sit on that rock and pray over my congregation. There is a lot of pain down there. It is a good thing that our God has big ears."

What a lesson: he has come to pray and he brings his son with him.

The period after confirmation is a most natural time to help children take an important step forward in prayer. Prior to the age of reason, we can and should teach vocal prayers to a child; but after the age of reason, and particularly into early adolescence when young people start to become more aware of their own subjectivity and capacity to set goals for themselves, we should also encourage in them a habit of mental prayer.

Parents are instrumental in helping their children acquire this habit by their encouraging words, by their example, and even by the priority they give each day to sharing a quiet time of prayer with their older child. Of course, it is virtually impossible to teach a child to do something that we don't do ourselves. So let's schedule some mental prayer daily. Just as friendship requires a sharing of hearts and minds, so too a habit of trusting, heartfelt prayer is a necessity for a deep relationship with God.

Yet, despite our best intentions, it can be a challenge to fit in personal prayer time. Prayer always requires some sacrifice, but those who do it find they still have time for other things, as these examples show:

- One young dad has decided there is only one way to fit in his twenty minutes of mental prayer: to get up at 5:15 so he can finish his prayer before his son gets up. The boy is already up and running around at 6.
- Another young husband reflects on this same challenge: "My wife and I decided that we would cut out entertainment on our personal screens. Now we both have more than enough time in the day, despite our newborn, to fit in time for prayer and some spiritual reading. This has been a big discovery for me."
- With the agreement of his wife, another man retreats to a quiet room on arriving home from work. There he has a habit of doing twenty minutes of mental prayer, often joined by his teenage sons, whom he invites to join him without ever hassling them.

There is much at stake. Without a habit of prayer to process our priorities, we are easily distracted by the "milk and honey."

We all need to *learn* to pray: Pope Francis insists, "Praying is something learned, just as we learn to walk, to speak, to listen."[3] But children are receptive to "the art of prayer," as St. John Paul called it.[4] As a school principal, I saw many children giving priority to quiet daily prayer in the school chapel, often on arrival at school, typically sitting for fifteen or twenty minutes in silent reflection, and often helped by a copy of the Gospels or another spiritual book. The essential thing is to give one's full attention. Our prayer is worth what our attention is worth.

Bedazzled

The Beatitudes assemble in one short passage the summary of the kingdom of heaven. In St. Matthew's Gospel they are the first words of the Sermon on the Mount. We are not meant just to pick one but to embrace all. They constitute a very practical teaching of Jesus about

3. Francis, Homily "Holy Mass with Priests, Men and Women Religious, Consecrated People and Seminarians" (February 16, 2016). Vatican website: https://www.vatican.va/content/francesco /en/homilies/2016/documents/papa-francesco_20160216_omelia -messico-religiosi.html.

4. John Paul II, Apostolic Letter *Mane Nobiscum Domine* (October 7, 2004), 8. Vatican website: https://www.vatican.va /content/john-paul-ii/en/apost_letters/2004/documents/hf_jp-ii _apl_20041008_mane-nobiscum-domine.html.

the mastery of our thoughts and actions that is required by true holiness.

But what comes next? Our Lord stresses that holiness must reach out to others:

> You are the salt of the earth. But if salt has lost its taste, how shall its saltness be restored? It is no longer good for anything except to be thrown out and trodden under foot by men.
>
> You are the light of the world. A city set on a hill cannot be hid. Nor do men light a lamp and put it under a bushel, but on a stand, and it gives light to all in the house. Let your light shine before men, that they may see your good works and give glory to your Father who is in heaven (Mt 5:13–14).

At the Sea of Galilee, when the sun rises on the eastern side over the dry Golan Heights, all becomes dazzlingly bright as the sun is mirrored in the water. Everything is changed. What was pitch black before is now overpoweringly brilliant. When Jesus said, "I am the light of the world (Jn 8:12)," everyone around the Sea of Galilee knew exactly what he meant. They witnessed the power of light to change everything. Jesus is that light, and he calls us to be as well. And at night, still visible from the shore is the "city set on a hill," the village of Safad, known as S'fath in biblical times. Our Lord used images that the locals understood to emphasize how each of us must bring light to family, friends, and colleagues.

We cannot be holy without being salt and light for others. One leads to the other. It is Jesus himself who links the call to holiness with the call to apostolate. Through the sacrament of confirmation we receive the courage and clarity to practice this unity of life.

Work With the Love of Jesus

We look to the sacrament of confirmation to give us the courage to stand by our convictions and faith, to speak up in charity, in season and out of season. One example is Gianna Jessen's 2008 testimony to parliament members in the Australian state of Victoria. It was on the eve of their vote on late-term abortion. It is possibly the most powerful speech you will ever see. Gianna Jessen survived a saline abortion. She speaks out of love not anger, but she does not mince words. She is a warrior for truth.

Despite the cerebral palsy with which she was left after she survived a failed abortion, Gianna has addressed millions in live audiences. She says,

> I'm invading the culture as an unconventional woman, just being me. The beautiful thing about having cerebral palsy is it's part of my sermon. It's my way of reminding the earth that heaven is real. My legs have become a net to act as a fisher of men.[5]

How can we raise children who are not afraid to speak up? Again, it is by example. Ask for a stronger faith. Let us not fear the world, nor those would howl us down. As Gianna once said, "I am God's princess and you don't mess with God's girl!"[6] This world is our turf and we should plant our flag firmly and insist that this world is God's turf. It is a gift from God our Father. Let us not deface it with sin.

The sacrament of confirmation equips us and our children with supernatural fortitude, turning all we do

---

5. Gianna Jessen (2016). Her personal website: http://giannajessen.com/.

6. "Gianna Jessen - Queen's Hall Melbourne speech 2008," YouTube video, posted by Zoran Veršec, October 28, 2013, https://www.youtube.com/watch?v=k-j-9yEAUc4&ab_channel=ZoranVer%C5%A1ec.

into love. "Perfect love casts out fear!" writes St. John (1 Jn 4:18). The more we love, the less we fear anybody and anything. Remember, love is a choice, not simply a feeling. It is a decision based on clear thinking and established habits of managing our timidity.

Mother Teresa herself wrote of Gianna:

> God is using Gianna to remind the world that each human being is precious to Him. It is beautiful to see the strength of the love of Jesus, which he has poured into her heart. My prayer for Gianna, and for all who listen to her, is that this message of God's love will put an end to abortion with the power of love.[7]

The gift of fortitude is there for us to use, but we need to exercise it. We can't leave it in the cupboard. The more we invest in our loving response to Jesus, the more he can fill us with his power. Let us pour out our hearts in daily loving prayer.

---

7. Teresa of Calcutta, Personal Letter (October 29, 1994), posted by Jessica Renshaw June 23, 2019. Website: https://hiddeninjesus .wordpress.com/2019/06/23/my-letter-from-mother-teresa/.

The Good That One Person Can Do

An example of someone who exercised an extraordinary influence through his ordinary work was Jan Tyranowski, a tailor who lived in Poland between the two world wars. If not for his selfless attention to the young Karol Wojtyla, it is possible that the world would never have received the great gift of St. John Paul. He himself wrote of Jan:

> He was one of those unknown saints. . . . He disclosed to me the riches of his inner life, of his mystical life. In his words, in his spirituality and in the example of a life given to God alone, he represented a new world that I did not yet know. I saw the beauty of a soul opened by grace.[8]

Arguably, this unknown man changed the history of the world, and he did this by starting a parish prayer group, The Living Rosary, and by offering spiritual guidance to the teenagers attending. One who was later ordained has stated that he and Karol Wojtyla owed their priestly vocations to this humble man.

8. Pope John Paul II, and André Frossard, *"Be Not Afraid!" Pope John Paul II Speaks Out on His Life, His Beliefs, and His Inspiring Vision for Humanity* (New York: St. Martin's, 1982), p. 18.

Jan was the epitome of ordinariness, but this ordinariness did not limit his effectiveness. Even when he contracted tuberculosis, his suffering was motivated by the desire to co-redeem with Christ. Complications from the amputation of his arm gave him excruciating pain and kept him in a hospital away from Karol's ordination, but he said, "I am lying here doing nothing, but I still want to work for the salvation of the world. . . . So I am offering up my pain for the benefit of all those in need— and for Karol as well."[9] He has been declared venerable by Pope Francis.

We all have the duty to lend a hand to our neighbors. Christians and pagans alike can see how important this is. Cicero proclaimed, "Men were brought into existence for the sake of men, that they might do one another good."[10] And the Roman schoolmaster Publilius Syrus reminded his pupils, "He who lives only for himself is truly dead to others."[11] We can teach children to do the same: on

---

9. As quoted in Jason Evert, *Saint John Paul the Great: His Five Loves* (Lakewood, CO: Totus Tuus, 2014), chapter 11.

10. Cicero, *De Officiis*, 1.7.22.

11. Publilius Syrus, *The Moral Sayings of Publilius Syrus, A Roman Slave*, trans. D. Lyman (Cleveland: L. E. Barnard, 1856), 771, p. 65.

Friday after work take your teenager out to help in a soup kitchen; on Saturday invite your daughter to bike over with you to visit an elderly parishioner; be quick to visit a friend who is grieving, help another friend move, and cut the grass or shovel the walk of your elderly neighbor. The corporal and spiritual works of mercy reflect the common duties we all share with our fellow human beings.

But the high point of the spiritual works of mercy is to sow in the lives of others a yearning for holiness and an understanding of how to get there. This was Jan's genius. St. John Paul insisted, "In virtue of Baptism the believer . . . is called to be holy and to collaborate in the salvation of humanity."[12] And at the top of the list is to do a first-rate job with your own children.

Sanctify Work

The Prussian chancellor Otto von Bismarck must bear a degree of responsibility for the militarization of Europe before the start of World War I. He is reputed to have

---

12. John Paul II, Homily "Canonization of St. Josemaría Escrivá de Balaguer" (October 6, 2002). Vatican website: https://www.vatican.va/content/john-paul-ii/en/homilies/2002/documents/hf_jp-ii_hom_20021006_escriva.html.

said that he had only three words of advice for young Germans: "Work, work, work."

Hard work *alone* is not a good thing. We can turn our work into prayer only with unity of life, only if we turn it into loving service. "God makes use of nothing other than love," wrote St. John of the Cross, a Doctor of the Church.[13] St. Josemaría would tell students and office workers, that their desks are like altars. It is there we offer our best to God. Mother Teresa said simply, "My love is expressed in my work."[14] And her namesake, St. Teresa of Ávila, insisted to those working in the kitchen that "amidst the pots and dishes remember that our Lord goes along with you."[15]

Dr. David Livingstone understood this. He started his professional life intending to be a missionary for the London Missionary Society. He ended it as an explorer,

---

13. John of the Cross, "The Spiritual Canticle," in *The Collected Works of St. John of the Cross*, 3rd ed., trans. Kieran Kavanaugh, OCD, and Otilio Rodriguez, OCD (Washington, DC: ICS, 1991), 28, p. 583.

14. Mother Teresa, as quoted in Kerry Walters "Mother Teresa: Love in Action," Franciscan Media website: https://www.franciscanmedia.org/franciscan-spirit-blog/mother-teresa-love-in-action.

15. Teresa of Ávila, *The Book of the Foundations*, trans. John Dalton (London: T. Jones, 1853), p. 27.

who integrated his missionary efforts and his medical care for others into all he attempted. He wrote,

> My views of what is *missionary* duty are not so con- tracted as those whose ideal is a dumpy sort of man with a Bible under his arm. . . . I am "not my own." I am serving Christ when shooting a buffalo for my men, or taking an astronomical observation.[16]

As a layman, he took full responsibility for his own actions: I "follow out my own plans as a private Christian."[17] And he applied initiative and creativity to the great task of raising up primitive and superstitious peoples. He proposed "God's highway" to the Royal Geographic Society—a plan to open up East Africa to non-exploitative commerce. He wrote, "I believe we can, by legitimate commerce in the course of a few years, put an entire stop to the traffic of slaves over a large extent of territory."[18] He realized that opening the country to honest trade would also open the country to Christianity.

---

16. Blaikie, p. 216.

17. Livingstone, as quoted in Tim Jeal, *Livingstone* (New York: Newsweek books, 1974) p. 69.

18. As quoted in Andrew C. Ross *David Livingstone: Mission and Empire* (London: Bloomsbury, 2002), p. 119.

There was no doubting his sense of mission and service, all expressed through arduous explorations into uncharted East Africa. And he grasped the need to be as personally prayerful as he could be, to facilitate his missionary work. On one occasion, despite being feverishly bedridden with jungle sickness for eighty-four days, he used the time to read the Bible four times from start to finish.

He died in harness on expedition. Despite mortal illness that had confined him to bed, he was found slumped over his bed; he had died kneeling in prayer.[19] His life demonstrates an exemplary integration of the human and divine.

Confirmation empowers us to be exemplary laymen and laywomen, determined to change this world for the better through our work, and to guide our children so they will do the same in their turn. Let us offer our work to God in the Mass and in our morning offering and prove the genuineness of this offering by not allowing our work to erode family life and prayer life, and by our concern for the spiritual welfare of those with whom we work.

---

19. Blaikie, p. 376.

Confirmation

Model these convictions, attitudes, and actions, and talk about them to your child:

- Faith
- Prudence
- Fortitude

Ages for principal focus on these goals: 7–14

Pray about these areas of example in your own life as a parent.

- Do I ask the Holy Spirit dwelling within my soul to guide me?
- Do I make use of the gifts of the Holy Spirit to help me imitate Jesus more perfectly?
- Do I focus my attention on God and others? Where do I let selfishness creep in?
- Am I determined to spend generous time in daily prayer?
- Do I generously give time to conversation daily with my spouse and each of my children?
- Do I try to be salt and light for others?
- Do I use my strength to do good? Or do I sometimes use it to pursue power, pleasures, and possessions?
- Do I look on my work as loving service?

Education of head: Sow these convictions in your child.

- I can talk to God in my soul.
- I set goals for myself.
- Sincerity is essential.
- Without generosity I cannot love others.
- Work is service.
- I should use my freedom, which is a great gift, to do what is good.
- I am loyal to my friends. I help them whenever they need a hand. I speak honestly to them.

Education of heart: Education of a child's desires and feelings.

- I trust God my Father when things are difficult.
- I want to make Jesus happy by spending time with him in prayer.
- I try not to give up or complain.
- I enjoy being with family and I don't isolate myself in my room or in headphones when there are family gatherings.
- I have discovered the joy that comes from helping others.
- I trust my parents and obey them, thank them, and ask their advice.

CHAPTER 4

Holy Eucharist

Every afternoon I went out for a walk with Papa, and we paid a visit to the Blessed Sacrament in one or other of the churches.

–Autobiography of St. Therese of Lisieux[1]

How much can the Eucharist inflame a life with faith, even if the recipient is a boy. Emmanuel Tohi was the oldest boy in his family. He was fifteen when he was diagnosed with a progressive illness that would take

---

1. Thérèse of Lisieux, *Autobiography of St. Thérèse of Lisieux*, chap. II, www.ccel.org/ccel/therese/autobio.x.html.

his life a year and a half later.[2] "We will storm heaven to get you better," his mother assured him. "That's good," he responded, "long as you say after each prayer, 'Thy will be done.'"

> He asked her, "Now that I am sick, can I go to Communion each day, and to Confession each week?" His mother from that point onward started taking him daily. Some months later he spoke to her, "Mom, if I don't get better, you won't stop going to Holy Communion each day, and to Confession each week, will you?" In those months of Emmanuel's terminal illness, he taught his parents and siblings so much about accepting the will of God and about love of Jesus in the Eucharist. His mother says simply, "I was a religion teacher, but he was the one teaching us."

In this section, where we look at passing on a love for the Eucharist, let us remind ourselves that it is the Holy Spirit who is in charge and who forms the heart and

---

2. Read the story of Emmanuel at: www.mn.catholic.org.au /news-events/news/in-the-end-i-am-so-proud-of-my-son/. Quotes contained here are from personal conversations with Emmanuel's parents.

mind of a baptized child. We are but the instruments. It is his curriculum, but let us be the best of teachers in this school of love.

God With Us

The philosopher Elizabeth Anscombe tells a charming story:

> I knew a child, close upon three years old and only then beginning to talk, . . . who was in the free space at the back of the church when the mother went to communion. "Is he in you?" the child asked when the mother came back. "Yes," she said, and to her amazement the child prostrated itself before her. I can testify to this, for I saw it happen.[3]

Her point is that even small children can grasp the fact that God is present in the Eucharist, and that the most natural response for us all is of gratitude and adoration.

---

3. G.E.M. Anscombe, *Transubstantiation* (London: Catholic Truth Society, London, 1974); reprinted in G.E.M. Anscombe, *Collected Philosophical Papers Volume III: Ethics, Religion and Politics* (Oxford: Blackwell, 1981), p. 108.

The Holy Eucharist

"The Most Blessed Eucharist contains the entire spiritual boon of the Church, that is, Christ himself, our Pasch and Living Bread, by the action of the Holy Spirit through his very flesh vital and vitalizing, giving life to men who are thus invited and encouraged to offer themselves, their labors and all created things, together with him."[4]

The Eucharist is the greatest of the sacraments. St. John Paul insisted, "The Church draws her life from the Eucharist."[5] And remember we are the Church.

The word *Eucharist* means thanksgiving. Gratitude is the fundamental attitude of a creature owing everything. The Holy Eucharist is the best way for us to give glory and offer thanksgiving to God.

Jesus explained to the apostles that his death was the sacrifice of a new covenant between God and men, the promise from God that he will never leave us. When we attend the Eucharistic sacrifice, we are transported to Calvary and we strive

---

4. Paul VI, Decree on the Ministry and Life of Priests *Presbyterorum Ordinis* (December 7, 1965), 5. Vatican website: https://www.vatican.va/archive/hist_councils/ii_vatican_council/documents/vat-ii_decree_19651207_presbyterorum-ordinis_en.html.

5. John Paul II, Encyclical Letter *Ecclesia de Eucharistia* (April 17, 2003), 1. Vatican website: https://www.vatican.va/content/john-paul-ii/en/encyclicals/documents/hf_jp-ii_enc_20030417_eccl-de-euch.html.

to respond with all of our attention, gratitude, and compassion.

Holy Communion is the "daily bread" that we ask for in the *Our Father*. When we receive Holy Communion, we consume the living Christ, "the soul is filled with grace and a pledge of the life to come is given to us (CCC 1402). "He who eats my flesh and drinks my blood has eternal life, and . . . abides in me and I in him" (Jn 6:54, 56). We believe that Christ is present—"his Body and his Blood, with his soul and his divinity" (CCC, 1413)—in each particle and drop. It is the resurrected and living Jesus that we receive, and who awaits us the tabernacle. Only the appearances of bread and wine remain. The *Catechism of the Catholic Church* refers to this change of substance as *transubstantiation* (n. 1376).

For these reasons we treat the Blessed Sacrament with extreme reverence. Those who distribute Holy Communion are either the priest or one to whom special authorization has previously been given. We should only receive Holy Communion if we are not aware of grave sin on our soul. St. Paul is very clear on this: "Whoever, therefore, eats the bread or drinks of the cup of the Lord in an unworthy manner, will be guilty of profaning the body and blood of the Lord" (1 Cor 11:27). The Church also asks us to adore the Blessed Sacrament before receiving, normally by bowing, and to keep the Eucharistic fast of one hour.

> Children should receive their First Communion soon after the age of reason, having been well instructed to distinguish the Eucharist from normal bread.

Yet, how easily we chatter, read the parish bulletin, or even check our phones when we are waiting for Mass to start. Pope Benedict wrote and preached a great deal on the Eucharist in his book, *God Is Near Us*:[6]

In life today, often noisy and dispersive, it is more important than ever to recover the capacity for inner silence and recollection. Eucharistic adoration permits this, not only centered on the "I" but more so in the company of that "You" full of love who is Jesus Christ, "the God who is near to us."[7]

St. John Paul urged in his conclusions to the Synod on the Laity, *Christifideles Laici*, that we should cling to Jesus. Pope Francis has the same message, that we be

---

6. The book is a collection of the pope's homilies. Benedict XVI, *God Is Near Us: The Eucharist, The Heart of Life*, ed. Stephan Horn and Vincenz Pfnür, trans. Henry Taylor (San Francisco: Ignatius Press, 2003).

7. Benedict XVI, Angelus (June 10, 2007). Vatican website: https://www.vatican.va/content/benedict-xvi/en/angelus/2007/documents/hf_ben-xvi_ang_20070610.html.

Christians "who confess Jesus with their lives because they hold him in their hearts."[8]

J. R. R. Tolkien, the author of T*he Lord of the Rings*, wrote of the "never-ceasing silent appeal of the Tabernacle" that the Eucharist inspired in him, a "sense of starving hunger," even though "out of wickedness and sloth I almost ceased to practice my religion." He stated simply, "I fell in love with the Blessed Sacrament from the beginning, and by the mercy of God never have fallen out again."[9]

In the great gift of the Fatima apparitions, we were reminded of the need for surpassing reverence for the Eucharist. The angel announced to the children in one of the earliest apparitions, "Take and drink the Body and Blood of Jesus Christ, horribly insulted by ungrateful man. Make reparation for their crimes and console your God."[10] We console our God when we receive him

8. Francis, Homily "Holy Mass and Blessing of the Sacred Pallium for the New Metropolitan Archbishops on the Solemnity of Saints Peter and Paul, Apostles" (June 29, 2017). Vatican website: https://www.vatican.va/content/francesco/en/homilies/2017/documents/papa-francesco_20170629_omelia-pallio.html.

9. J.R.R. Tolkien, Letter to his son Michael Tolkien (November 1, 1963), as quoted in *The Letters of J.R.R. Tolkien* (Melbourne: Allen and Unwin, 1981), p. 340.

10. William Thomas Walsh, *Our Lady of Fatima* (New York: Doubleday, 1990), p. 42.

well, but we insult him grievously when we receive him unworthily, in mortal sin, or in indifference.

The gratitude that should be in our hearts was well captured by one young mother who asked her husband returning from a retreat, "And could you visit the chapel any time of night? How lucky!"

Privilege

Newly baptized adult Catholics can help us see the Eucharist with new eyes. I had the privilege of meeting Caleb in upstate New York in 2012. He was a thirty-year-old father of two, completing his nursing qualifications. His teenage years, however, had been rather unbridled and drug-fueled. He put his story on paper for my students:

> My impression of Christians was that they were very judgmental and thought they were better than everyone else. I remember coming home drunk and stoned and very late only to find the house locked. I slept out front in the grass and awoke the next Sunday morning. I had never been up that early

on Sunday, but I saw all the churchgoers in suits and nice clothes getting in their cars and giving me disgusted looks. These were my neighbors, I didn't even know them, they had never taken the time to get to know me or help me for that matter. Deep down inside I knew I needed help, and no one seemed to want to give it. I felt like Christianity was a cold religion and that Christians lived in their own bubble.

Deeply worried about his son, Caleb's father introduced him to a Protestant pastor-friend. Soon Caleb had become a Christian and was working in youth ministry. Four years later he went to China as an underground Protestant missionary and worked there for eight years. On return, he discovered his best friend had become Catholic and entered the seminary. "After much study, prayer, and argument" this friendship led him, and his wife, to the Catholic church:

One thing that struck me most during my (Protestant) conversion experience in 1997 was that the preacher kept insisting that God dwells within us. It was this message that made me hungry that night and has kept me hungry ever since. One thing that struck me most during my (Catholic) conversion experience in 2010, was that the priest kept insisting that I was going to receive Jesus, God incarnate, in the Eucharist, and not just part of Jesus, ALL of Jesus. "In Him the whole fullness of deity dwells bodily" (Col 2:9). Are you hungry for God?

See, in our prayer and in our worship of Him, we not only begin to know Him, we become one with Him. In a sense we also become Him to the world, we are His Mystical Body. Like Mary, we also become His Temple. When people see His Temple they hunger for relationship, when they see Him, they bow down in adoration. Let people see Christ in you.

The Real Presence of Jesus Christ in the Eucharist is the most precious privilege bestowed on the Catholic Church. This privilege is not like the honor of visiting a great person, but the all-encompassing reality of owing everything to God, of being lifted up, of receiving life. It is Jesus himself who talks of the Eucharist as lifegiving. If we eat his flesh we possess "eternal life". No mean promise!

Pope Benedict captures this concept beautifully: "The

human creature . . . is . . . endowed with an extraordinary dignity. . . . He finds himself able to enter into communion with God."[11] Yet we can frustrate this divine plan.

There is no shortage of testimonies from the saints about the Eucharist. St. Thomas Aquinas, greatest of Catholic theologians, insisted that the Eucharist is the highest of the sacraments—"the end of all the sacraments"[12]—but it the phrase generally attributed to St. Pius X, with his gift of practical advice, goes, "Holy Communion is the shortest and safest way to heaven."

"Why Don't They Believe?"

A Honduran bishop was speaking emphatically at the 50th World Eucharistic Congress in Dublin. "Why don't they believe in the Eucharist?" he asked, before providing his own answer. "They don't believe because they are not educated to believe in the Eucharist."[13] Yet this education

---

11. Benedict XVI, General Audience (May 4, 2011). Vatican website: https://www.vatican.va/content/benedict-xvi/en/audiences/2011/documents/hf_ben-xvi_aud_20110504.html.

12. *Summa*, III.73.3.c.

13. The author was present during the bishop's speech. 50th World Eucharistic Congress, Our Lady Queen of Peace Parish, Merrion Road, Dublin (June 15, 2012).

is assured when a parent feels the great duty to teach a child to recognize, accompany, and depend on the great realities of the Eucharist and the Mass.

Scripture could not be clearer. The Old Testament prefigures the great miracle of the Eucharist through the supernatural gift of manna to sustain the Hebrews, and through the Ark of the Covenant whereby God accompanies his people. Jesus himself prepares his followers with the great miracles of the loaves and fishes, with blunt insistence that "I am the bread of life" (Jn 6:35), and "unless you eat the flesh of the Son of man and drink his blood you have no life in you" (Jn 6:53). He chooses the solemn eve of the Cross to institute the Eucharist, thus linking the Eucharist to his sacrifice. On the road to Emmaus he reveals himself at the breaking of the bread as at the Last Supper, and he refers to the Eucharist when he promises at his ascension, "I am with you always, to the close of the age" (Mt 28:20).

The early belief of the Church could not be clearer. In 115 AD, as he was being taken to Rome in chains to be fed to the lions, St. Ignatius of Antioch, wrote to the Christians of Smyrnea that they should not be influenced by those who "Do not confess that the Eucharist is the flesh of our Saviour Jesus Christ."[14] This was the belief of the first followers of Our Lord and it remains our belief.

It would be almost nine centuries before Jesus' presence in the Eucharist would be seriously challenged from within the body of Christians. That woeful distinction is accorded to Ratramnus (d. 868), a French monk at the Abbey of Corbie, who challenged his abbot, St. Paschasius (785–860), by insisting that Christ's body in the Eucharist differs from his body now in heaven. And from that point onward, every age has had its deniers. In the 1500s the Protestant reformers for the most part repudiated the Real Presence of Our Lord. In Protestant England, for example, in 1548 the words of the consecration were changed to remove any notion of an objective presence of Jesus. In 1550 the altars in all churches were removed and replaced by communion tables. And in 1558, within two weeks of her predecessor's funeral, Elizabeth I forbade the elevation of the host at consecrations across England.

---

14. Ignatius of Antioch, "The Epistle of St. Ignatius of Antioch to the Smyrnaeans," trans. Charles H. Hoole (1885), chap. 6, www .earlychristianwritings.com/text/ignatius-smyrnaeans-hoole.html.

Even among Catholics today there are widespread misconceptions about the Eucharist. It is too easy to rationalize our way around miracles, turning the Body and Blood of Christ into "holy" bread. But when we deny that the Eucharist is Jesus himself, we sell God short—we decide that Jesus could not be *that* good; he could not love us *that* much. To deny the Eucharist is to deny the omnipotence and the goodness of God. Therefore, all effective catechesis of children must be deeply Christ-centered and emphasize the Real Presence of Jesus Christ, true God and true man, in the Eucharist, with his Body, Blood, soul, and divinity.

Let us never lose sight of the Mass as "Christ's covenant of love with the Church."[15] Let's think about this. The old covenant between God and the Jewish people was a promise of mutual fidelity, sealed by the blood of bulls sacrificed in the temple. Jesus says that his death is the new covenant, sealed with his own blood, once for all time, whereby, as St. Peter writes in his second letter, God "has granted to us his precious and very great promises,

---

15. Thomas J. McGovern, *The Most Holy Eucharist: Our Passover and Our Living Bread* (Nashua, NH: Sophia Institute Press, 2013), p. 147.

that through these you may escape from the corruption that is in the world because of passion" (2 Pet 4).

The Mass, as the renewal of the new covenant, was prophesied by the prophet Malachi: "For from the rising of the sun to its setting my name is great among the nations, and in every place incense is offered to my name, and a pure offering" (Mal 1:11).

Such "precious and very great promises" are not to be scoffed at. The *Catechism of the Catholic Church* draws on the classic phrase of St. Athanasius, "God became Man so that man might become God," to elaborate on this idea.

> The Word became flesh to make us *"partakers of the divine nature"*: "For this is why the Word became man, and the Son of God became the Son of man: so that man, by entering into communion with the Word and thus receiving divine sonship, might become a son of God." "For the Son of God became man so that we might become God." "The only-begotten Son of God, wanting to make us sharers in his divinity, assumed our nature, so that he, made man, might make men gods."[16]

---

16. *Catechism of the Catholic Church*, 460.

To be "divinized," let us stand by his cross in the Mass and share his cross in our daily sacrifices. His suffering on our behalf must not be far from our thoughts. So, when Pope Francis says, "when we go to Mass it is as if we're going to Calvary itself,"[17] he is also reminding us that we cannot separate the Eucharist from the passion of Jesus. Jesus himself urges us to celebrate the Eucharist as a memorial of his passion. Compassion is a virtue and we must show compassion too to our God. We must not leave him alone on the cross.

Memory of the great generosity of others makes us more grateful. Jesus said, "Do this in remembrance of me" (Lk 22:19): what we keep in our thoughts reveals what we value. We cannot live our lives so immersed in the everyday present that we forget what our parents, our loved ones, and most of all our God have done for us. God the Father says to Catherine of Siena in her extraordinary *Dialogue*, a treasure of the Church, "I provided you with the gift of memory so that you might hold fast

---

17. Francis, General Audience, (November 22, 2017). Vatican website: https://www.vatican.va/content/francesco/en/audiences/2017/documents /papa-francesco_20171122_udienza-generale.html.

my benefits and be made a sharer in my own, the eternal Father's power."[18]

Pope Benedict taught that the Mass is "the greatest and highest act of prayer."[19] In the Mass Christ is praying, offering his suffering for our redemption and spiritual needs. When we go to Mass, we unite ourselves, and all our works and challenges, with his offering. For this reason the Mass is the perfect place to offer our work to God and to pray for souls. St. Josemaría insisted, "Keep struggling, so that the Holy Sacrifice of the Altar really becomes the center and the root of your interior life, and so your whole day will turn into an act of worship—an extension of the Mass you have attended and a preparation for the next."[20]

Attending daily Mass with loving devotion is a highway to holiness. This is the experience of young and old of all times.

18. Catherine of Siena, *The Dialogue,* trans. Suzanne Noffke, O.P. (Mahwah, NJ: Paulist Press, 1980), p. 277.

19. Benedict XVI, Homily "Holy Mass for the Ordination to the Priesthood of Deacons of the Diocese of Rome" (May 3, 2009). Vatican website: https://www.vatican.va/content/benedict-xvi/en /homilies/2009/documents/hf_ben-xvi_hom_20090503_ordinazioni -sacerdotali.html.

20. Josemaría Escrivá, *The Forge*, (Scepter: 2002), 69.

Antiquity of the Mass

Without the Mass there can be no Eucharist. The *Catechism of the Catholic Church* presents the realities as virtually interchangeable.[21] The Mass is the Eucharist, though from a different perspective. The Mass refers to the action of Our Lord offering himself to the Father and our union with that sacrifice. Normally, when we speak of the Eucharist we refer to the Body and Blood of Christ, the living Christ, given to us in Communion at Mass. Therefore let us treasure the Mass.

Because the Eucharist dates from the time of Christ, it is not surprising that we have descriptions of the Mass from the first decades of Christianity. The Mass was already essentially in its current form from before 150 AD. St. Justin Martyr gives us a summary of the Mass liturgy by that date. There is a reading from both Old and New Testaments, a sermon, the prayer of the faithful; the wine is mixed with water as it is today; the bishop leads a long thanksgiving prayer including petition (in which the consecration takes place) and the whole congregation

---

21. See *Catechism of the Catholic Church*, 1328-1332.

answers "Amen," as they still do today, at the end of the Eucharistic prayer; and Holy Communion is distributed. There is even a kiss of peace, the forerunner to our current sign of peace.

The liturgy of the Mass drew on Old Testament Jewish ritual and other aspects of Jewish life. Christ instituted the Eucharist in the middle of a Jewish family meal, hence in the Mass all takes place under the leadership of the head of the house: the bread is broken, the bread and wine are blessed, and there is a long thanksgiving prayer. The Prayer of the Faithful and the "Holy, holy, holy" prayer before the canon are also both adapted from early Jewish rituals.

In the early 200s, St. Hippolytus of Rome describes so much of what we are familiar with every Sunday. The whole Second Eucharistic Prayer, almost verbatim, was composed by Hippolytus. He describes the priest extending his hands over the gifts through the whole of the Eucharistic Prayer; the priest dialogues with the congregation during the preface; he repeats our Lord's words, "Do this in memory of me" (the *anamnesis*); he calls down the Holy Spirit to sanctify the gifts (the *epiclesis*); he concludes the Eucharistic Prayer with the solemn doxology:

"Through Him, with Him, in Him." When offering Holy Communion, the priest would say *"Panis caelestis in Christo Jesu"* (The bread of heaven in Christ Jesus), to which the communicant would answer "Amen."

Other aspects of the Mass are also very much in evidence in the first centuries: Tertullian (ca. 155–220) makes reference to the psalms that are recited between the readings, our current responsorial psalm; the Kyrie was adapted by the Roman church from the Eastern liturgies; the Creed dates from the Council of Nicaea in the early 300s; and the Gloria was based on an early Christian hymn adopted in the Mass during the 300s. Much of our current First Eucharistic Prayer also dates from the 300s.

It is also in the historical record that already in the 200s, daily Mass was customary in African dioceses. On fast days, the congregation would eat nothing until after the ninth hour (3 PM), when the Mass was celebrated, timed to coincide with the time Our Lord died.

Why is all this significant? To appreciate and participate in the Mass are duties of love for a Catholic. Without the Blessed Sacrament we lose our direct and tangible connection to what Our Lord has done for us. Let us pass this on to our children.

The Language of the Blessed Sacrament

Even a disoriented, dying woman can understand the Eucharist as otherworldly food. After weeks of undiagnosed restlessness, one very elderly lady was told there was nothing that could be done except to keep her comfortable. She was moved to a hospice in the inner suburbs of Sydney. The lunch trolley came rattling along the corridor, and then there was a knock on the door of her room, "My dear, would you like some food?" She immediately responded, "Give me some heavenly food."

The Eucharist is food for eternal life. This is the fundamental message our Lord wishes us to understand. Indeed we should all focus on this heavenly food. St. John records Christ's words:

He who eats my flesh and drinks my blood has eternal life, and I will raise him up at the last day. For my flesh is food indeed, and my blood is drink indeed. He who eats my flesh and drinks my blood abides in me, and I in him (Jn 6:53–56)."

Food gives life. St. Augustine writes, "If you receive the Eucharist properly, you are what you have received."[22] The life of Christ is given to us in the Eucharist, that we "may have life and have it abundantly" (Jn 10:10). As a sacrament, the Eucharist fulfills the very language of its symbolic imagery. And this changes our life in the present. "The wonder we experience at the gift God has made to us in Christ gives new impulse to our lives and commits us to becoming witnesses of his love."[23]

The bread and the wine were foreshadowed in the Old Testament by the offering of bread and wine by Melchizedek, who makes a cameo Old Testament appearance but leaves his mark. So many other images and prophecies of the Old Testament prepare us for the sacrifice of Calvary and its renewal in the Mass. Continuous animal sacrifices were offered in the temple to seal the covenant with God. The original paschal lamb was instrumental to the escape from Egyptian slavery.

---

22. Augustine of Hippo, *Sermon 227*, as found on The St. Anselm Institute for Catholic Thought website: https://stanselminstitute.org/files/SERMON%20227.pdf.

23. Benedict XVI, Post-Synodal Apostolic Exhortation *Sacramentum Caritatis* (February 22, 2007), 85. Vatican website: https://www.vatican.va/content/benedict-xvi/en/apost_exhortations/documents/hf_ben-xvi_exh_20070222_sacramentum-caritatis.html.

The blood of the lamb, marking the lintels of the Israelites' homes, saved them from the angel of death. The blood of Jesus, the Lamb of God, according to St. John the Baptist, seals the new covenant.

And let us remember that Jesus Christ is God and man. He understands the importance for human beings to be physically present to those they love. It is not the same to talk on the phone as to talk face-to-face. We all know that. We long for the physical presence of those close to us. Jesus longs to be with us, and the Eucharist makes this possible. The Church applies to our Lord in the Blessed Sacrament the words of the Old Testament, where God is found "delighting in the sons of men" (Prv 8:31).

Furthermore, the language of Holy Communion is of complete self-donation. Our Lord gives himself to us totally, and we hand ourselves over in return: "It is no longer I who live, but Christ who lives in me" (Gal 2:20). This is the language of love. Love seeks union: "that they may be one even as we are one, I in them and thou in me, that they may become perfectly one" (Jn 17:22–23).

The Eucharist gives us a glimpse of heaven where the complete self-giving of our God to us will be fully realized. "No eye has seen, nor ear heard, nor the heart of man conceived, what God has prepared for those who love him," (1 Cor 2:9)

How is it that we are not more grateful?

Learn to Yearn

Let's revisit Caleb. With Caleb's permission, I invited my senior students to send him questions to answer. One asked, "What is your motivation in practicing your faith now?" He answered simply, "The Eucharist." Another asked, "What do you see in the Eucharist?" He answered,

> The question is who? I see none other than Jesus Christ. He gives all of Himself to us . . . 100%. He is a jealous lover, He wants all of us . . . 100%. This is what it means to be a saint . . . to give Him 100%. I still have a long way to go . . . God help me.

In answer to another question, he wrote about depth of prayer before our God in the Eucharist.

> Let me share something I have learned to do recently at Mass and at Eucharistic Adoration. Christ dwells in the tabernacle. Mindfully submit your whole life to Him in worship. I try to lay

out all my struggles, worries, wants, needs, joys, thanks, and anything I can't think of before Him and say, "Thy will be done" or, "Let it be done to me according to Your word." It doesn't always have to be emotional. We must remember faith goes beyond appearances and even emotions. Often times I don't feel anything but the pain and numbness in my knees from kneeling down for so long. Now, take that abandonment and walk with it outside. Take it with you when you play sports, when you spend time with friends, when you labor at your schoolwork, when you do your chores, when you fall ill, when you are ridiculed, when you are praised, when you fall and when you get up. Simply say it again and again, "Thy will be done." And remember "in everything God works for good with those who love Him" (Romans 8:28). Let your life be your worship and give thanks for He is Good!

I was confident Caleb's answers to questions were going to be good, but I hadn't realized they would be this good.

Prayer in front of the Eucharist should not be an optional extra. St. John Vianney said in one of his simple and heartfelt sermons:

If we really loved the good God, we should make it our joy and happiness to come and spend a few moments to adore Him, and ask Him for the grace of forgiveness; and, we should regard those moments as the happiest of our lives.[24]

We read in St. Paul that we must live "in" Christ. He uses this expression no less than sixteen times in the first two chapters of Ephesians alone, explaining that when we live simply according to natural appetites, we are dead men. Hence, we must crave the things of God.

But we cannot live "in God" and live for our own goals. To the Romans he wrote, "To set the mind on the flesh is death but to set the mind on the spirit is life and peace . . . for if you live according to the flesh you will die, but if by the Spirit you put to death the deeds of the body you will live" (Rom 8:5, 13). One or the other has to go.

We are called to think Jesus' thoughts, to model our lives on him, to be Christ to others. Christ "died for all, that those who live might live no longer for themselves but for him who for their sake died and was raised" (2

---

24. John Vianney, "18th meditation" in *Eucharistic Meditations* (New York, Scepter Publishers, 2016), p. 96.

Cor 5:15). We must become *identified* with him, to live his life: "It is . . . Christ who lives in me" (Gal 2:20). In other passages, St. Paul explains that to be identified with Christ is to live the life of the Spirit. "For those who live according to the flesh set their minds on the things of the flesh, but those who live according to the Spirit set their minds on the things of the Spirit" (Rom 8:5). And simply, "Have this mind among yourselves, which was in Christ Jesus" (Phil 2.5), and to have this mind is to live his life (see Col 3:1-10).

St. John Paul said that God has "no other hands but ours." Our task is to do God's work. For this he strengthens us: "The Holy Spirit strengthens in each the inner man so he finds himself in a sincere gift of self," St. John Paul writes in *Dominum et Vivificantem*.[25] And he pre-enables all efforts with grace. "For we are his workmanship, created in Christ Jesus for good works, which *God prepared beforehand*, that we should walk in them" (Eph 2:10, emphasis added).

---

25. John Paul II, Encyclical Letter *Dominum et Vivificantem* (May 18, 1986), 59. Vatican website: https://www.vatican.va/content /john-paul-ii/en/encyclicals/documents/hf_jp-ii_enc_18051986 _dominum-et-vivificantem.html.

How can we dispose ourselves to receive this grace of living in Christ and doing his work? The simplest and most direct path is to draw strength from the Eucharist. We must yearn for the Eucharist. If we strive to place the Eucharist at the center of our lives, we are the great beneficiaries. Bishop Javier Echevarría put it strikingly: "Our Eucharistic piety determines the value of our life."[26]

Woman of the Eucharist

It will be in our last words and actions that our abiding loves are revealed. St. John Paul's last major writings focused on the Eucharist and its life-giving necessity for the Church. At the end of 2002 he had issued a letter inaugurating the Year of the Rosary and establishing the Luminous Mysteries, the last of which is the Institution of the Blessed Eucharist. His only encyclical letter in the new millennium, in 2003, was about the Eucharist, entitled *Ecclesia de Eucharistia*, and it started with the words, "The Church draws its life from the Eucharist."

26. Javier Echevarría, "Pastoral Letter for the Year of the Eucharist" (October 6, 2004). Opus Dei website: https://opusdei.org/en-us /article/partorial-letter-for-the-year-of-the-eucharist/.

He described Mary as the "Woman of the Eucharist," noting her "profound relationship" with the Eucharist.

> Is not the enraptured gaze of Mary as she contemplated the face of the newborn Christ and cradled him in her arms that unparalleled model of love which should inspire us every time we receive Eucharistic communion?[27]

One year later in *Mane Nobiscum Domine* ("Stay with us Lord"—the words of the disciples on the road to Emmaus), he proclaimed for the whole Church the Year of the Eucharist from October 2004 to 2005. He returned again to the importance of contemplation of Jesus in the Eucharist and to how the Rosary can help us immensely in this.

> Let us deepen through adoration our personal and communal contemplation. . . . The Rosary . . . will prove a particularly fitting introduction to Eucharistic contemplation, a contemplation carried out with Mary as our companion and guide.[28]

---

27. John Paul II, *Ecclesia de Eucharistia*, 55.
28. John Paul II, *Mane Nobiscum Domine*, 18.

Apart from a shorter letter about the role of technology in evangelization, this was his last major writing.

Pope Benedict continued this exploration into the association of Mary with the Eucharist. In 2007 he wrote:

> Consequently, every time we approach the Body and Blood of Christ in the eucharistic liturgy, we also turn to her who, by her complete fidelity, received Christ's sacrifice for the whole Church. The Synod Fathers rightly declared that "Mary inaugurates the Church's participation in the sacrifice of the Redeemer." She is the Immaculata, who receives God's gift unconditionally and is thus associated with his work of salvation. Mary of Nazareth, icon of the nascent Church, is the model for each of us, called to receive the gift that Jesus makes of himself in the Eucharist.[29]

In Jerusalem the chapel of the Cenacle is the closest Catholic oratory to the site of the Last Supper. The altarpiece is a striking bronze sculpture of the institution of the Eucharist. The apostles are gathered around Jesus. The tabernacle is within the sculpture, placed at the very

---

29. Benedict XVI, *Sacramentum Caritatis*, 33.

heart of our Lord. Standing at the side of the sanctuary is Mary, gazing lovingly and serenely at her son. The image is most beautiful. What a joy for the pilgrim to discover, in this most sacred space linked to the Last Supper itself, that Mary goes before us, lovingly contemplating Jesus and the Blessed Sacrament. Let us imitate her.

Blessed Eucharist
Model these convictions, attitudes, and actions, and talk about them to your child: • Charity • Gratitude
Ages for principal focus on these goals: from 3 or 4 upwards
Pray about these areas of example in your own life as a parent. • Am I awestruck by Jesus' love for us in the Blessed Sacrament? • Do I show my gratitude by a time of thanksgiving after receiving the Eucharist? • Do I visit and adore the Blessed Sacrament daily? • Do I attend Mass whenever it is possible, and do I follow the prayers closely? • Do I speak the language of the Blessed Sacrament—total gift of myself to those I love? • Do I ask Jesus to transform me so I can be "Christ to others"?

- Do I teach my children to ask Mary to keep me close to her Son?
- Am I a "Eucharistic soul" who strives not to forget that if we have shared in his cross we will share in his resurrection? (see Rom 6:5).

Education of head: Sow these convictions in your child.

- Jesus is present in the Blessed Eucharist in our tabernacles. We should keep him company.
- Jesus comes to us in Holy Communion so that we can grow in strength and love. We must be so grateful.
- We adore Our Lord in the Blessed Sacrament because we owe him everything.
- The Mass allows us to be present on Calvary. We attend with gratitude, awe, and reverence.

Education of heart: Education of a child's desires and feelings.

- To be with our Lord should give us greatest joy.
- I please our Lord by receiving him well.
- I thank our Lord after Holy Communion in the deepest and most loving prayer of my week.
- To be able to adore our Lord in the Blessed Sacrament is a great privilege.
- I am aware of the great privilege to be able to be present at Calvary in a mystical way at Mass.
- I show my love for Jesus on the cross by honoring and kissing the cross in my room.

CHAPTER 5

Penance and Reconciliation

He who conceals his transgressions will not prosper, but he who confesses and forsakes them will obtain mercy.

—Prv 28:13

Right behind the Eucharist as a sacrament we can receive frequently is penance. Also known as reconciliation, this sacrament enables us to recognize our faults, sins, and evil inclinations and through their confession, receive God's forgiveness and obtain the grace to struggle more effectively to follow Jesus in all our actions.

The saints have time and again emphasized the importance of regular confession, down through the ages. St. Louis IX of France wrote to his son, the future Philip III:

> Dear Son, I advise you that you accustom yourself to frequent confession, and that you choose always, as your confessors, men who are upright and sufficiently learned, and who can teach you what you should do and what you should avoid. You should so carry yourself that your confessors and other friends may dare confidently to reprove you and show you your faults.[1]

Catherine of Siena urged monthly confession at the very least.

> You must . . . if you wish your soul to preserve grace and grow in virtue, to make your holy confession often for your joy, that you may wash your soul's face in the Blood of Christ. At least once a month,

---

1. Louis IX, "Letter of Saint-Louis IX, *Roi et Confesseur*, to his Son Philip III." Christendom Restoration Society website: http://www.christendomrestoration.org/uploads/9/0/2/6/9026344/letter-of-st-louis-ix-to-his-son.pdf.

since indeed we soil it every day. If more, more; but less it seems to me ought not to be done.[2]

St. John Paul's love for confession is virtually legendary. He would go to confession weekly and also before big feast days. As a bishop he lined up with other faithful for confession. Just months before his death he wrote, "It would be illusory to desire to reach holiness—according to the vocation that each one has received from God—without partaking frequently of this sacrament of conversion and sanctification."[3]

The Gift of Peace

Jason Evert, in his *John Paul the Great*, tells of an occasion when the Pope had invited a group of priests to eat with him, and one brought with him a fallen-away priest who was now homeless in Rome. John Paul asked him to hear

---

2. Vida Dutton Scudder, trans. & ed., *Saint Catherine of Siena as Seen in her Letters* (London, New York: J.M. Dent & E.P. Dutton, 1905). Dominican Central Archives website: www.domcentral.org /trad/cathletters.pdf.

3. Catholic News Agency, "Pope says frequent Confession needed to achieve holiness," March 28, 2004, www.catholicnewsagency.com/ news/867/pope -says-requent-confession-needed-to-achieve-holiness.

the Pope's confession. He hesitated because he said that permission had long ago been taken from him. John Paul reminded him that as pope he had the power to restore to him that right. He heard the Holy Father's confession, and he then asked for confession in return. The Pope then commissioned him to care especially for the destitute.[4]

The sacrament of confession has the power to grant an extraordinary inner peace because of our confidence that God has forgiven us—even if it is not necessarily carried out in the proper way.

Confession brings such peace of heart. For this reason, Sydney's Archbishop Anthony Fisher calls it "the sacrament of liberation."[5] The gift of the sacrament of confession arrives in the very first appearance of our Lord to his disciples on Easter Sunday.

Jesus came and stood among them and said to them, "Peace be with you." When he had said this, he showed them his hands and his side. Then the disciples were glad when they saw the Lord. Jesus said to them again, "Peace be with you. As the Father has sent me, even so I send you." And when he had said this, he breathed on them,

4. Evert, *Saint John Paul the Great: His Five Loves*, p. 190.

5. Archbishop Anthony Fisher, Homily, Wollemi College (April 6, 2011).

PENANCE AND RECONCILIATION ◆ 119

and said to them, "Receive the Holy Spirit. If you forgive the sins of any, they are forgiven; if you retain the sins of any, they are retained" (Jn 20:19–23).

Joy is a very natural result when, through sincerity, we remove an obstacle between ourselves and another. If we have the faith to see God as our loving Father, we find our peace restored when we get to confession. And faith is a question of prayer. What we ask for we get.

The Sacrament of Penance and Reconciliation

"Three conditions are necessary for Penance: contrition, which is sorrow for sin, together with a purpose of amendment; confession of sins without any omission; and satisfaction by means of good works."[6]

Jesus was born to "save his people from their sins" (Mt 1:21). Our Lord's first words in his public life were "Repent, and believe in the gospel" (Mk 1:15). Repentance is a prerequisite to everything else. When we humble ourselves to admit our faults, we find faith easier and have already started to pray again.

Old Testament teachings also emphasize the need we have of God's pardon: "Bring us back to

6. Thomas Aquinas, *The Aquinas Catechism: A Simple Explanation of the Catholic Faith by the Church's Greatest Theologian* (Nashua, NH: Sophia Institute Press, 2000), p.86.

you, Lord, that we may return" (Lam 5:21). Eze-
kiel reminds us that true repentance includes
the effort to reform one's life: "But if the wicked
man turns away from all the sins he has committed, if he keeps all my statutes and does what is
just and right, he shall surely live. He shall not
die!" (18:21).

After his redemptive passion, Jesus' first gift
to the Church was the life of grace, and the sacrament of penance, so that all could remain in the
graces he had won for us: "Receive the Holy Spirit.
If you forgive the sins of any, they are forgiven; if
you retain the sins of any, they are retained." On
Easter Sunday evening he appeared to the apostles, who had locked themselves away, showing
them his wounds and announcing that he was giving them a mission. "Peace be with you. As the
Father has sent me, even so I send you." This mission came with the power to forgive sins.

Humility Wins

Another route to confession comes from the prompting of
those closest to us. A businessman found himself let down
by a supplier and was drawn into an angry discussion on
the phone. Just as he let loose a particularly expressive
word, he looked up to see his ten-year-old staring at him
in shock. The boy turned and walked out.

Next Sunday, standing at the back of the church, his son looked up at him and said, "Are you going to confession?"

"Do you think I need to?"

The boy nodded and said, as encouragingly as he could, "I'll go with you if it helps."

How well this father had raised his son, and with what humility he accepted his son's advice, went to confession, and spoke with pride to his friends at his son's daring.

Humility is a *sine qua non* for every relationship, and most of all for a relationship with God, our Creator and Father. Without humility, we can justify practically anything, and behave in ways catastrophic for ourselves and for others. St. John writes bluntly, "If we say we have no sin, we deceive ourselves, and the truth is not in us" (1 Jn 1:8). When we hurt someone else, that relationship can only be fixed by a heartfelt admission of our mistakes and by reforming our behavior. We all need to say we're sorry. On both a human and a supernatural level, repentance makes sense.

The virtue of humility is about grasping the reality of our situation as a creature, and about acknowledging our need to put things right with our God and others. It falls under the umbrella of prudence. C.S. Lewis stated that the man who is humble will not be thinking about humility, "he will not be thinking about himself at all."[7] We must focus our life on others if we want to be humble.

Let us not forget that confession is a great act of humility. Pope Francis speaks of confession as a "sacrament of joy." He urges young people not to remain prisoners of shame for sins, for "God is never ashamed of you. He loves you right there, where you are ashamed of yourself. And He loves you, always."[8] Shame can be a positive experience that leads us to God.

The Rite of Confession

The Catholic Church teaches that individual confession is the only ordinary way by which a person can be reconciled with God and the Church after committing a serious sin. For a valid confession, we need to fulfill the three parts of the sacrament: contrition (sorrow for our sins, or at least for the punishment from God that our sins

---

7. C.S. Lewis, *Mere Christianity* (New York: Harper One, 2009), book 3, chap. 8, Kindle.

8. Francis, Apostolic Journey to Slovakia: Meeting with Young People (Sept. 14, 2021). Vatican website: https://www.vatican.va /content/francesco/en/speeches/2021/september/documents /20210914-kosice-giovani.html.

deserve), confession of our sins, and satisfaction (completing the penance after the confession)

1. After a greeting, the penitent makes the Sign of the Cross, and the priest invites the penitent to have trust in God.
2. The penitent says words to the effect: "Bless me Father, for I have sinned. It has been [length of time] since my last confession." (The Church requires us not to leave the confession of a mortal sin more than a year. By what is known as the "Easter duty," we should receive Holy Communion at least once between Ash Wednesday and Trinity Sunday, and therefore go to confession as necessary to be in the state of grace.)
3. The penitent makes a concise confession of serious sins as accurately as we are able. We should ask for the priest's help if necessary. The Church recommends we confess not only mortal sins but also venial sins and actions whereby we have put ourselves voluntarily and in an unjustified way into temptation. These are called "occasions of sin."
4. The priest may offer advice and guidance.
5. The priest proposes a penance to be completed.
6. The penitent recites an act of contrition; for example, "Lord Jesus, be merciful to me a sinner."

7. The priest imparts absolution, for which the essential words are, "I absolve you from your sins in the name of the Father, and of the Son, and of the Holy Spirit."
8. The priest invites the penitent to give thanks and to go in peace.

Closer Despite Everything

A shopkeeper rang a school principal to say he had caught a student shoplifting. The boy was eleven years old.

"Leave it with us," the principal said.

The next morning the principal spoke to the boy. "Alex, your dad needs to know about this." Alex went white. The principal later forewarned the boy's rather volatile father, "Alex has something to talk to you about tonight. Hear him out."

Next day the father called back. "Thank you. My son and I had the best talk we have ever had. Alex grew six inches last night." All was put right, and the son had apologized to the shopkeeper in the presence of his father. It seemed like a big win.

But something even better was coming. When Alex left school eight years later, his class was asked to note down the single best memories of their entire school life. Alex wrote about his conversation that night with his father. (Don't we all have a very deep need to own up to our faults?) And of course, the father, by showing the restraint he did, turned this episode into a life-changing event.

Reread the beautiful parable of the prodigal son (Lk 15:11–32). Jesus, who knows, is telling what the Father is really like: "No one knows the Father except the Son and any one to whom the son chooses to reveal him" (Mt 11:27). The story shows the great mercy of the Father, and that, with humility, sincerity and repentance, we are *closer* to God *after* reconciliation than we were *before* we sinned. How remarkable. The prodigal son completely squanders his inheritance on loose living, but on return he is not only closer to the father than before he sinned, but he is closer than the brother who considered himself sinless and superior. What do we conclude? To acknowledge our sin and our unworthiness is what matters. When there is humility, God's mercy draws us closer than ever.

This is not an isolated message. To humble ourselves is the condition of repentance. Time and again we are shown that if we admit the reality of our unworthiness, God picks us up and embraces us. The centurion says, "Lord I am not worthy to have you come under my

roof" (Mt 8:8), and immediately his servant is cured. The
Syrophoenician woman compares herself to a dog eating
scraps from the floor, and immediately her daughter is
healed (Mk 7:24–30). The thief on the cross says, "We
are receiving the due reward of our deeds" (Lk 23:41),
and he is promised paradise. Peter says, "Depart from
me, for I am a sinful man, O Lord" (Lk 5:8), and Jesus
makes him the Prince of the Apostles. And the contrary
is also illustrated: the Pharisee standing at the front of
the temple who draws attention to his fasting but whose
prayer is self-satisfied goes away unreconciled to God
(Lk 18:9–14).

St. John Paul ensured that the first canonization of the
new millennium was to be of St. Faustina, through whom
the devotion of Divine Mercy was given to the world.

> Sr. Faustina's canonization has a particular elo-
> quence: by this act I intend today to pass this mes-
> sage on to the new millennium. I pass it on to all
> people, so that they will learn to know ever better
> the true face of God and the true face of their breth-
> ren. In fact, love of God and love of one's brothers
> and sisters are inseparable, as the First Letter of
> John has reminded us: "By this we know that we

love the children of God, when we love God and obey his commandments" (5: 2).[9]

We sell God short. We think he could not be merciful to the point of wiping away our sin and coming to us as spiritual food. Surely God is not that good! Yes, he is, and to mistrust God's mercy is to lack faith. Jesus says as much to the woman: "Your faith has saved you; go in peace" (Lk 7:50).

Mesmerized by the Shroud

The last two years of the lives of Hans and Sophie Scholl, the young anti-Nazi dissidents, were marked by their rising indignation at the perversity of the regime, along with waves of personal self-doubt and discouragement. During this time they were buoyed up by the discovery of Christianity and prayer through their meeting with a seventy-year-old Catholic intellectual, Carl Muth, through a young Catholic friend. Muth had been banned

---

9. John Paul II. Homily "Mass in St. Peter's Square for the Canonization of Sr. Mary Faustina Kowalska" (30 April 2000). Vatican website: https://www.vatican.va/content/john-paul-ii/en/homilies/2000/documents/hf_jp-ii_hom_20000430_faustina.html.

from lecturing by the Nazis, and so he gathered discussion groups in his home, inviting Hans and Sophie. Later Hans offered to help him in his library and Sophie occasionally helped too. There they came across a book about the Holy Shroud of Turin, regarded by many as the authentic burial pall of Christ.

Just under fifty years before, in 1898, the cloth, with its faint sepia bloodstains, had been photographed by an Italian, Secondo Pia. His negatives greatly enhanced the image, revealing unsuspected detail of the suffering figure it had enwrapped and bringing the shroud to the world's attention. His photos clearly showed the gaping wounds in the hands and the side, trickles of blood from the crown of thorns, the trails of blood down the arms as they hung from the nails, and the barbarous scourging extending around the shoulders and thighs. The most skeptical observers were obliged to admit that the wounds bore an inexplicable resemblance to those of the Christ.

Quickly the shroud became the subject of forensic interest. There is no doubt that it is the actual burial shroud of a man who died exactly as Christ died. The blood stains are real blood, and yet the nature of the image defies scientific analysis. The nail wounds in the wrists, in contrast to usual and almost universal conventional representations placing the nails in the palms of the hands, have been shown to be anatomically accurate if nails are to hold the weight of a body.

The detailed history of the cloth may be traced only to the 1300s, but sound hypotheses piece together its path in prior centuries. The herringbone weave is the same as that of contemporaneous tombs in the Middle East. Pollen embedded in the shroud is unique to the Holy Land. And in more recent decades studies have even revealed that the eyes of the victim were closed, according to known customs of the time, by coins from the time of Christ. Amazing.[10]

The photographs were a momentous discovery for Hans and Sophie. Both were convinced the images were indeed of Christ after his passion. Sophie wrote, "I'm surprised the picture doesn't cause more of a stir, considering that Christians can't but regard it as the face of God, perceptible to their very own eyes."[11] She spent long periods of time gazing at what she believed to be an image of the

10. Scientists have contradictory data from carbon testing of the shroud. Some tests suggested a dating from the 1300s, but such anomalies can be explained by fires that have damaged parts of the fabric and also by handling of the cloth over so many centuries.

11. As quoted in J.P. Holding, *Hitler's Christianity* (Tekton, 2013), Kindle.

dead Christ. Her prayer life flourished. She felt that the shroud made God accessible.[12]

Like Hans and Sophie, many today hold that the shroud is indeed a relic of the dead Christ. Dr. Pierre Barbet's *Doctor at Calvary*, with its medical analysis of the shroud, has further helped generations to grasp the enormity of our Lord's passion.[13] He found evidence of paired hooks, most likely of bone, tipping the thongs of the scourge. His detailed analyses showed the consistency of the images with both scripture and with the effects of death by crucifixion, and his study of the congealing blood even offered insights into Christ's slumped posture on the cross after death. All is on display. We can only look in compassionate reverence and pray. St. Paul reminds us, "You were bought with a price. So glorify God in your body" (1 Cor 6:20). To look upon the shroud is to meet Jesus in his sacred humanity, and to respond with compassion to his sufferings and with sorrow for one's own sins.

The Church reveres the holy humanity of Jesus, that he is truly man and that he really suffered. His pain is real.

12. Ruth Hanna Sachs, *White Rose History, vol. 1: Coming Together* (Lehi, UT: Exclamation!, 2003), p. 593.
13. Pierre Barbet, *A Doctor at Calvary* (New York: P.J. Kenedy, 1953).

His love is real. At the very start of his first letter, John speaks of "That which was from the beginning, which we have heard, which we have seen with our eyes, which we have looked upon and touched with our hands, concerning the word of life" (1 Jn:1). Remember that emotion is a powerful motivator. When a child starts to comprehend the suffering of our Lord, they will have taken into their lives a massively important principle in relation to our faith: that love entails true sacrifice.

This is a lesson accessible even to a small child. I was at the home of a friend when his two-year-old daughter came into the room with a children's picture book about the Passion. She showed us the nails in Jesus's hands and said, "Ouch." The infant was rerunning times that her parents had shown her the pictures, given a simple explanation, and reacted in just this way. How wise were these parents. Let us never doubt the importance of modeling compassion for our Lord's suffering, and of holding conversation with a small child.

The Great Evil of Sin

To pay attention to the wounds of our Lord is to be moved by his willing suffering on our behalf. And so we better grasp the great evil of sin.

The words of the angel at Fatima, and of Mary herself, give us further insight into the gravity of sin. Lucia, the oldest of the children, described the third apparition of the angel. Some months before he had already appeared urging them to pray in reparation for sin. This time, when he comes, he finds them playing during the midday siesta. One would think that it would be reasonable for six-, eight- and nine-year-olds to be playing at their lunchtime, but the angel speaks urgently to them:

> Suddenly, we saw the same Angel right beside us. "What are you doing?" he asked. "Pray! Pray very much! The Hearts of Jesus and Mary have designs of mercy on you. Offer prayers and sacrifices constantly to the Most High."
>
> "Make of everything you can a sacrifice, and offer it to God as an act of reparation for the sins by which He is offended, and in supplication for the conversion of sinners. You will thus draw down peace upon your country. I am its Angel Guardian, the Angel of Portugal. Above all, accept and bear with submission, the suffering which the Lord will send you."[14]

---

14. Louis Kondor, ed., *Fatima in Lucia's Own Words II* (Fatima, Portugal: Secretariado dos Pastorinhos, 2016), p. 79.

The children started immediately to pray the prayer they had been taught: "My God, I believe, I adore, I hope, and I love You! I ask pardon of You for those who do not believe, do not adore, do not hope, and do not love You!"

Soon Our Lady herself appeared to them. In the third of the apparitions, in July, she spoke of the great need to pray for sinners, and of the coming of a second world war, as a terrible consequence of sin.

> Sacrifice yourselves for sinners, and say many times, especially whenever you make some sacrifice: O Jesus, it is for love of You, for the conversion of sinners, and in reparation for the sins committed against the Immaculate Heart of Mary.
>
> You have seen hell where the souls of poor sinners go. To save them, God wishes to establish in the world devotion to my Immaculate Heart. If what I say to you is done, many souls will be saved and there will be peace. The war is going to end; but if people do not cease offending God, a worse one will break out during the pontificate of Pius XI.

Finally, Mary gave the children the prayer that we now say between the decades of the Rosary.

"When you pray the Rosary, say after each mystery: O my Jesus, forgive us, save us from the fire of hell. Lead all souls to Heaven, especially those who are most in need."

Then, looking very sad, Our Lady said:

"Pray, pray very much, and make sacrifices for sinners; for many souls go to hell, because there are none to sacrifice themselves and to pray for them."

What are we to make of this? First, we are left in no doubt about the horror of sin and of the need to pray in reparation; and second, we see how we must strive to totally avoid mortal sin, and deliberate venial sin which predisposes us to mortal sin. St. John Paul spoke of the necessity of prayer if we are to change our lives: "It is in prayer that the Holy Spirit transforms our lives."[15] The answer is prayer: "Pray that you may not enter into temptation," Jesus urged (Lk 22:40). Let us do our best to cooperate with grace, making our best efforts to change

---

15. John Paul II, Homily "Holy Mass in Pontcanna Fields" (June 2, 1982). Vatican website: https://www.vatican.va/content/john-paul-ii/en/homilies/1982/documents/hf_jp-ii_hom_19820602_cardiff.html.

our behaviors, avoiding situations where we know from sad experience that we can fall into sin.

Teach Right From Wrong

Parents of every age and culture have felt a parental duty to give moral guidance to their children. Essentially this is formation of conscience. Consider this father who, caring deeply for his son, passed on unforgettable life lessons.

At twelve years of age, in the early 1980s, Yichen was being trained in a secret corps of Chinese child soldiers destined to become an elite army battalion. Only the fact that his eyesight was not perfect saved him. When he was prescribed his first glasses, he was dumped from the program.

His father had been aloof from his upbringing, but when Yichen left for university at seventeen, his father wrote to him. "My son, now that you are leaving home, I need to say three things to you. Do not gamble. Do not take drugs. And do not play around with sex because you will need to be faithful to the woman you marry."

Thirty years later, Yichen still treasures the message. He has never forgotten it, and strives to live up to it.

A good conscience is necessary for good choices. For the ancient Greeks, knowledge of the difference between right and wrong was regarded as a mark of maturity: "I know the difference between right and wrong," insisted Telemachus, son of Odysseus, when he asked permission of Penelope to leave in search of his missing father.[16] What better gift could a parent offer than authentic moral and religious education that leads to personal convictions? But how few parents offer this in a comprehensive way!

The core business of conscience is to judge whether our proposed actions are genuine expressions of love of God and others. Pope Francis writes of how easily our conscience falls dormant when there is not love.[17] Teach your children that love is the measure of every action. Actions are not good because of the feelings they evoke but because they are genuinely focused on what we owe others—in the first place to God. To forgive others is the condition on which we can be forgiven: "Forgive us our trespasses, as we forgive those who trespass against us."

---

16. Homer, *The Odyssey*, trans. E.V. Rieu (London: Penguin, 1976), p. 282.

17. Francis, *Solo l'amore ci può salvare* (Vatican City: Vatican Publishing House, 2013), p. 83.

In *Evangelii Gaudium* Francis also warned us against a blunted conscience that accompanies "the desolation and anguish born of a complacent yet covetous heart [and] the feverish pursuit of frivolous pleasures."[18] Milk and honey are everywhere to be found! The prodigal son had blunted his conscience because all his attention was on his own self-indulgence. Only when the pleasures disappeared was he free from their grip. Therefore it is so important that young people are formed from an early age to say no to self-indulgence.

So let us teach children to do a simple examination of conscience each night. "Commune with your own hearts on your beds," we are told in Psalm 4, and St. Augustine taught, "Examine yourself without self-deception, without flattery. . . . You must be dissatisfied with the way you are now if you ever want to get to where you are not yet."[19] A simple daily examination is a must, lest we are blind to

---

18. Francis, Apostolic Exhortation on the Proclamation of the Gospel in Today's World *Evangelii Gaudium* (November 24, 2013), 2. Vatican website: https://www.vatican.va/content/francesco /en/apost_exhortations/documents/papa-francesco_esortazione -ap_20131124_evangelii-gaudium.html.

19. Augustine, *Sermons: Works of Saint Augustine* Part III, translated by Edmund Hill, OP (New York: New City Press, 1991), Sermon 169, 15.

our faults like Mr. Darcy in *Pride and Prejudice*, who said, "I have been a selfish being all my life, in practice, though not in principle."[20]

What is a good method? Start by asking the Holy Spirit for light and spend three minutes in reflection on the day. Examine particularly where we have been self-centered in our thoughts and actions, make a heartfelt apology, and make a resolution for tomorrow. It's that simple. Here is how a great theologian of the twentieth century sums it up:

> We must ask for divine light . . . we ought every evening to search out with humility and contrition the faults that we have committed in thought, word, deed, and omission . . . looking fixedly at God (the soul) should ask itself how the Lord himself will judge its day, or the week just spent. In what has it been entirely his? In what entirely its own? In what has it sought God sincerely? In what has it sought itself?[21]

---

20. Jane Austen, *Pride and Prejudice* (Boston: Little, Brown and Company, 1892), p. 543. Available at: https://archive.org/details/prideprejudice0000aust_c5r0/page/n9/mode/2up?q=selfish.

21. R. Garrigou-Lagrange O.P, *The Three Ages of the Interior Life, Vol 1* (Rockford Illinois: Tan Books, 1989), p.304-5.

Two or three minutes is all that is needed. Even sit with a young child to teach them how to do this. Start with a prayer to the Holy Spirit asking for light. Teach them to look at their duties to God (prayer, offering up their work with love of God, versus self-indulgence, vanity), and their duties to others (loving others as Jesus would love them, avoiding unkindness, dishonesty, and so on). Make a simple resolution for tomorrow, and finish with an act of contrition that is also an act of love of God.

Children Love What We Love

Can a parent be the decisive influence on the faith of each son and daughter? Is this asking too much? Can a parent pass on a love of the sacrament of confession? Try to establish customs of talking often and deeply.

We can learn from the example of the elder Karol Wojtyla, who took early retirement from the army when his wife died. Karol, his son and future pope, was eight. Thereafter he and his son would go for long walks daily after school. Where did the young Karol develop his love of his faith, his piety, his love of music and culture, his dramatic sense, his capacity for hard work, his idealism and responsibility for others, even his patriotism? If his father had not taken such close care of his development, would we have St. John Paul II, with his so marvelously rounded character despite all the privations of the war? Probably not. History has shown that by his diligent parenting, the father served his country far better than by holding a rifle.

What is the lesson? Formation is personal. Talking one-on-one is priceless. We all must learn to open our hearts. Unless your son and daughter share with you what they are thinking and experiencing, there can be no education worth the name. (Remember *education* is of the mind, and *training* of the emotions of a child.) Think of all your efforts to protect your child from bear pits in the cyber world. Sheltering is so necessary but has a used-by date. During the window of adolescence, unless your teen talks to you about his or her experiences online, you will not be able to coach cyber self-control. The same goes for their social life. And the same for their life of prayer. We have little knowledge of what is happening in the life of a teenager if they do not tell us. The aim is to build habits of communication, not one-offs.

"What's your secret?" I asked the father of an admirable family. His three boys were well-respected in their school. They were tenacious sportsmen, elected leaders of their respective classes, open and honest, and hardworking students. Their family is close and the children love their father and mother. The father reflected on my question, and said,

> When my oldest was about thirteen, I needed to correct him about some behavior I noticed. When I spoke to him, I was very proud of him because he had tears in his eyes. I thought to myself, "What a good heart!" But after a week, when the behavior started to come back, I thought to myself, "This is not *my son's* fault. He has a good heart. This is *my* fault. I must give him more support." From that moment I have tried to talk weekly with each of my boys, helping them have a goal for the week ahead.

The results are there for all to see.

But remember that words and example go hand in hand. A father's son was going on an overseas holiday. Following the normal advice of the Church to confess before journeys and operations, the father was keen to see his son receive the sacrament before leaving. His son agreed, and he took him to the local church at the time of confessions on a Saturday afternoon. As his son got out of the car, he said, "You're coming too, aren't you, Dad?"

"Children love what we love" is a golden rule of parenting. This is true too in passing on our faith. So how do we pass on a love for the sacrament of reconciliation? By loving it ourselves. And how will your child know you love the sacrament? Because you talk about it positively, you use it often, and your child sees that going to confession gives you joy. And then follow another golden rule, "Schedule it or it won't happen."

Parents who talk about ideals and behavior, but without joy, leave their children in the invidious position of thinking, "I love you, and you keep telling me about the importance of confession, or prayer, or Mass, but these things don't seem to make you happy. I need things in life that will make me happy. Sorry."

Sacrament of Penance and Reconciliation
Model these convictions, attitudes, and actions, and talk about them to your child:
• Justice • Humility • Sincerity
Ages for principal focus on these goals: seven years and upwards

Pray about these areas of example in your own life as a parent.

- Do I know how to say sorry to those I love?
- Do I know how to forgive others? Does my difficulty in forgiving others ever lead me to think that God my Father may not forgive me?
- Do I love the sacrament of confession as a personal meeting with Jesus?
- Is my confession contrite, clear, and complete?
- Do I show the happiness that confession brings?
- When I look at a cross, do I think of all that our Lord has suffered for me?
- Do I do a daily examination of conscience? Am I deeply sorry for my sins?
- Am I determined to pass on a love for confession to each of my children?

Education of head: Sow these convictions in your child.

- To be in the state of grace is the greatest gift. I must not endanger this.
- I avoid deliberate venial sins and deliberate occasions of sin.
- God does not expect me to be perfect, only that I strive to be sorry for my faults.
- God my Father awaits me lovingly in confession.
- God's mercy is amazing. When we confess our faults humbly, we are closer to him than before our mistakes.

- "When I am weak then I am strong." Even when I try to do my best, I sometimes fail. God gives me the help of his grace most readily whenever I ask.

Education of heart: Education of a child's desires and feelings.

- Saying sorry makes me happy. I know I am not perfect, and I don't want to pretend I am.
- I have discovered the joy of regular confession.
- The cross is a reminder of all that our Lord has done for me.
- Humility helps me to serve others joyfully. I try to put myself last.
- I am so grateful to Jesus in my prayer for his constant help in the sacrament of confession.
- I share with my friends my love of confession.

CHAPTER 6

Anointing of the Sick

But well for him
that after death-day may draw to his Lord,
and friendship find in the Father's arms!

—BEOWULF

CA. AD 700[1]

B y the age of twenty, in 1940, Karol Wojtyla , the
future St. John Paul, had lost his father and mother,

---

1. *Beowulf*, trans. by Frances B. Gummere (Charlotte, NC: Duke
Classics, 2012), 3:71-3. MIT website: www.mit.edu/~jrising/webres
/beowulf.pdf.

his older brother, and his grandparents. So many of his friends, classmates, and the priests whom he knew had also died. He himself had just suffered a fractured skull, which left him close to death. The culture and faith of his homeland were being snuffed out. And yet, a biographer notes, "The pain of his father's death had opened up immense spiritual depths."[2]

Too often we look with the world's eyes. In this chapter we look at suffering through other eyes; through the eyes of St. John Paul, who taught that the highest motivation for suffering is love."[3] If our homes are to be schools of love, let us look on any suffering as a path to love.

Timeless Realities

Daniel was a boy whom I knew well because he had been a student at a small new school where I was teaching. As a ten-year-old, Daniel suffered for twelve months with non-Hodgkin's lymphoma before the disease took him. We thought of him as our first graduate, in the truest sense of the word. Daniel was supported by much prayer

2. Jason Evert, *Saint John Paul the Great* (Lakewood, CO: Totus Tuus Press, 2014), chap. 1, Google Books.
3. John Paul II, *Salvifici Doloris*, 30.

in his year of illness, first of all the prayer of his parents. In his last months it was apparent that his life was extraordinarily transformed, seemingly by an almost mystical union of his suffering with Christ's. His father spoke of entering Daniel's room when he was sleeping restlessly. Daniel explained, "Dad, I can't dream about anything except our Lord on the cross."

A few weeks before he died, a most extraordinary conversation took place. He asked his father:

"Dad, who was that prophet that took his son up the mountain?"

"Do you mean Abraham, Daniel?"

"Yes, Abraham. Dad, if God asked you to do that, what would you say?"

He was preparing his father not only for what was to come, but to accept God's will no matter how hard it would be. Daniel's father spoke of this conversation in his eulogy at Daniel's funeral. "I told Daniel that I didn't think God would ask that of me, but he has. But he has given us something very great in return: Daniel in heaven praying for us."

That heartbroken father's faith would be vindicated in the following years, just like the Old Testament patriarch's faith was vindicated. There came astounding blessings for his family and for Daniel's classmates. Among them were that the family received another boy born on the birthday of Daniel, five years later, a boy who was even the remarkable image of Daniel in appearance; and that some years later, Daniel's class each met personally with St. John Paul II.

How important for parents to talk of heaven, to foster in their own hearts and in the hearts of their children a yearning for heaven. What a marvelous incentive! It is said that St. Teresa of Avila, with the earnest valor of a small child, set off with her even younger brother to seek martyrdom, encouraging him with constant reminders that heaven is forever and forever.

Let's talk simply to children, without fostering fear, of the possibility that we could miss out if we are not sorry for our sins. Our Lord himself spoke clearly of hell, and said that many take the road to perdition. Nor does St. Paul pull punches. In one of his last letters he wrote of the tragedy of the loss of a soul, but also of the glorious hope of heaven.

> For many, of whom I have often told you and now
> tell you even with tears, live as enemies of the cross
> of Christ. Their end is destruction, their god is the

belly, and they glory in their shame, with minds set on earthly things. But our commonwealth is in heaven, and from it we await a Savior, the Lord Jesus Christ, who will change our lowly body to be like his glorious body, by the power which enables him even to subject all things to himself (Phil 3:18–21).

Knowing there is a radar trap ahead is not a guarantee that we will not get caught, but forewarned is forearmed.

Telegrams From Heaven

The following stories depicting the great kindness of our God accompanying his faithful friends in their last hours on this earth are unforgettable.

The family had just finished the Rosary in the downstairs family room after dinner. The grandmother in a lounge chair said simply, "I'm going up now." A grandchild jumped up to help her get out of her seat. She smiled, affectionately repeating, "I'm going up now. I love you," and with those words she shut her eyes and breathed her last.

Such extraordinary graces are perhaps more common than we think.

Anointing of the Sick

"By the sacred anointing of the sick and the prayer of priests the whole Church commends those who are ill to the suffering and glorified Lord, that he may raise them up and save them. And indeed she exhorts them to contribute to the good of the People of God by freely uniting themselves to the Passion and death of Christ."

Vatican II
Lumen Gentium, 11.

Even a life-threatening illness is a providential time to grow in holiness. On his last international journey, St. John Paul addressed the sick at Lourdes: "With you I share a time of life marked by physical suffering, yet not for that reason any less fruitful in God's wondrous plan."[4]

Perhaps no one more eloquently than St. John Paul has taught, in his life and in his words, the value of suffering that is accepted with love: "Prayer joined to sacrifice constitutes the most powerful force in human history."[5] His 1984 apostolic letter, *On the Christian Meaning of Human Suffering*, insists that suffering in union with God's will brings

---

4. John Paul II, Speech "Greeting of John Paul II to the Sick" (August 14, 2004). Vatican website: https://www.vatican.va/content/john-paul-ii/en/speeches/2004/august/documents/hf_jp-ii_spe_20040814_malati-lourdes.html.

5. Evert, *Saint John Paul the Great: His Five Loves*, p. 178. Quote is from a general audience given January 12, 1994.

us to holiness and releases love in the world. His own peace of heart as he descended into Parkinson's was evident to all. He joked, "Everyone else has a mobile phone, I have a mobile chair!"[6]

When we accept and offer up suffering, it is redemptive. We follow in the footsteps of Christ himself walking to Calvary: "I rejoice in my sufferings for your sake," wrote St. Paul (Col 1:24). The art form is of course to accept serious suffering with faith, and the sacrament of the anointing of the sick helps us greatly to do this.

"In the Anointing of the Sick we find a loving preparation for the journey which ends in the Father's house," wrote St. Josemaría.[7] Words in the Epistle of St. James point to its origins in Jesus' teaching: "Is any among you sick? Let him call for the elders of the church, and let them pray over him, anointing him with oil in the name of the Lord; and the prayer of faith will save the sick man, and the Lord will raise him up; and if he has committed sins, he will be forgiven." (Jas 5:14—15).

Theresa, an elderly Chinese lady, and her then-fiancé were each sentenced to twenty-five years in Chinese prison as political prisoners because they were in the Legion of

6. Caroline Pigozzi, *Pope John Paul II: An Intimate Life: The Pope I Knew So Well* (New York: Faith Words, 2008), p. 237, as quoted in Evert, *Saint John Paul the Great: His Five Loves*, p. 197.

7. Josemaría Escrivá, *Christ is Passing By*, no. 80.

Mary. Her crime was worse because she had written to their deported French parish priest. On release they both came to Australia, married, and dedicated themselves to teaching the faith to Chinese families. They would attend Mass daily. When her husband was in his eighties, he announced to his wife, "The thing I would like most of all is to die when I have received Holy Communion." The next day they were at Mass and came back to their seats after Communion. A few moments later she looked to her husband beside her and realized he had received his wish, his "telegram from heaven."

The Rite of Anointing of the Sick

If possible, the recipient should have reached the age of reason, and first receives the sacrament of penance and Reconciliation. Then the minister, who is a priest or bishop, anoints with holy oils the hands and forehead, saying,

"Through this holy anointing may the Lord in his love and mercy help you with the grace of the Holy Spirit. May the Lord who frees you from sin save you and raise you up."

If death is close, the person then receives *viaticum*, the Eucharist as bread for the journey to eternal life.

> The sacrament brings sanctifying graces and specific sacramental graces that unite us with Christ in his redemptive passion, bring us peace and trust in God, and forgive venial sins (and mortal sins if the person is repentant but unable to go to confession). As for all sacraments, preparation helps us to draw the greatest spiritual benefit, although this sacrament may be administered to an unconscious person in danger of death. At times too there are remarkable improvements in the person's physical health.

Let us not fear death. Death is our pathway to God. Pope Benedict insisted in *Spe Salvi*, his encyclical on hope, "When we pray we have hope."[8] If we wish to have a stronger faith and hope, we must have daily habits of prayer. If we wish children to understand that death is the gateway to heaven, we must form them in habits of prayer.

To act like this is to imitate Jesus, who prays with constancy in the face of death, teaching us to do the same. In what is known as his priestly prayer at the Last Supper, he prays at some length that the Father be glorified,

---

8. Benedict XVI, *Spe Salvi*, sec. 32.

and for those who have been entrusted to him. He leads the apostles in singing psalms before they leave for the garden, where it is his heartfelt prayer that the will of his Father be fulfilled. As he suffers, he prays for his executioners and recites psalms; and even his last words are a quotation from Psalm 31: "Into thy hand I commit my spirit" (31:5).

Pope Benedict spoke of this urgency to pray: "Prayer is not an accessory or 'optional,' but a question of life or death. In fact, only those who pray, in other words, who entrust themselves to God with filial love, can enter eternal life, which is God himself."[9]

God Asks a Lot of Us

Jeremy, twenty-seven, died in a snowboarding accident. He was self-effacing, popular, a very talented musician and sportsman. He breezed through university and had the world at his feet. The funeral was huge, perhaps six hundred—mostly former students from his school. One

---

9. Benedict XVI, Angelus (March 4, 2007). Vatican website: https://www.vatican.va/content/benedict-xvi/en/angelus/2007/documents/hf_ben-xvi_ang_20070304.html.

of the eulogies was delivered by a friend who had been with him on the slopes that day. "Jeremy always used to say, 'It gets better in the end, so if it's still bad, it's not the end.'" Therefore, we trust God's will, because in the end, God knows how to balance the books. Let us get out of our heads that because we get sick, or because bad things happen, that God is not paying attention.

Life *can* be very difficult, but no loving father gives his child a hard time for its own sake. If God, our most loving Father, asks so much of us, puts us through such a wringer in the natural course of life and death, how good must heaven be? Let us think back to our own childhoods. Good memories will totally eclipse the letdowns in a normal childhood; in the light of eternity, could it be that all the difficulties we will experience on the day we leave this world may have less significance than having to go to bed the night before our best holiday? And who remembers that?

These difficulties can only be infinitesimal in proportion to the inconceivable eternity that God wants to share with us, but nevertheless the pain and the suffering help us to win that eternity. They are a genuine sharing in the salvific Cross of Christ, if we turn these difficulties into trusting prayer.

Leading the Way

Is it not the natural duty of parents to teach children to cope with sufferings? Did St. Joseph glimpse something of this in his final illness, as he gave Jesus himself the example of embracing the will of the Father? Let us teach children that nothing happens by chance, that Jesus keeps us in his care, and there is no better place for us to be.

I think of that Paul whom I described earlier, who was a veterinary researcher and one of my oldest friends. His wife, Margaret, taught in the local Catholic school. I would stay with them on my trips to conferences in northern New South Wales before and after Paul's diagnosis with motor neuron disease. Damien and Kathryn, both still at school, saw their father bear his challenge with great strength. Even in his advanced illness he continued his work as a veterinary scientist.

Paul told me in one conversation that his goal was to become much closer to Jesus Christ. Several times he traveled to Sydney to be with Bethlyn, his oldest daughter, who was at university, and together they went to Mass. She helped him to walk, because, in this progressive disease, first mobility becomes a challenge, and then the use of upper limbs is lost as well. Finally it becomes harder to speak, to swallow, and ultimately, even to breathe. He bore his illness with admirable peace of soul and left his wife and children precious memories of how they were able to care for their father whom they loved very much. They saw it as a privilege. In Bethlyn's eulogy she said, "The disease robbed Dad of his dignity, his ability to move, to speak, to eat and breathe, and limited his participation in his passions. But it never robbed him of his ability to love." The great psychiatrist and holocaust survivor, Victor Frankl, the author of *Man's Search for Meaning*, put it this way: we can bear any "how" if we have a "why." Faith gives us a why.

Love brings patience—the virtue of being at peace amid suffering. Our emotions will not rebel against our reason when it looks on pain with faith and trust. Love brings joy even in suffering. This was the experience of the family of Stephen, who suffered an aggressive relapse of a cancer. Despite his own deteriorating condition, his wife's loss of her own parents, and a legal dispute with a neighbor, he texted on Christmas Day to his friends: "We are celebrating Christmas with joy. It is great to have such a major celebration at this time to take us from our troubles."

Without faith, suffering can seem a cruel and senseless plight, arbitrary and therefore unfair. With faith we can take up our cross each day, knowing that the cross is redemptive and that we can become another Simon of Cyrene, mysteriously lightening Jesus' cross. St. John Paul talked of how the Cross exposes the weakness and limitations of reason.[10]

Suffering is not the greatest evil. Even suffering that we fail to transform into love of God and others is but a lost opportunity, and tomorrow is always a new day, a chance to reset. The greatest of evils would be the loss of our soul. Suffering can unite us to Jesus and turn us back to God. We can turn our suffering into a prayer of reparation for our faults and the faults of others. Rob, a buoyant and confident self-made man in his early sixties, when asked how his chemotherapy was going, replied simply and humbly, "I have much to make up for."

The Holy Innocents

Nothing tests the faith of a parent more than the death of a child. Even then our example is crucial. The following texts are from James, the father of beautiful Jacob, who

10. John Paul II, Encyclical Letter *Fides and Ratio* (September 14, 1998), 23. Vatican website: https://www.vatican.va/content/john-paul-ii/en/encyclicals/documents/hf_jp-ii_enc_14091998_fides-et-ratio.html.

passed away from sudden infant death syndrome (SIDS). They are a testimony to how God our Father sustains us in a crisis.

> 8:17 AM Hi guys. Please pray for Jacob.
> He's not breathing. . . .
> Ambulance on the way.

> 8:51 AM Hi guys, Jacob passed away, probably for a few hours. Last time Jill saw him was when he last fed at 4.30am. Still got a big smile from him and then went peacefully back to sleep, then taken back to God. Thank you for your prayers and support. We really appreciate it.

> 1:52 PM Thanks so much everyone for your prayers and support. Please don't forget it's Frank's birthday today. Jacob is already partying in heaven.

Later that afternoon, immensely sad, yet at peace, Jill said, "We raise our children for heaven. What a blessing that Jacob is spotless and has gone straight to heaven. Our job is done with Jacob." She was grateful for a visit from a friend only two days before, who she felt was truly providential in preparing her. The friend spoke in detail of the death of her brother's child of SIDS the previous year. So Jill said, "When James called to me this morning in an urgent voice, God had already prepared me."

The outcomes are heart-wrenching, yet God's hand is patently present. Steve and Kim texted their friends after Anna Therese died soon after birth:

> A private family funeral is tomorrow. Little Anna Therese was born at 11:15 this morning. I baptized her and Fr. Max arrived shortly after and confirmed her (Mary of the Cross). The kids got here a couple of minutes later and all had the opportunity to hold her and say goodbye. Anna is now with her Father in heaven. Thank you for all the prayers.

Sometimes, too, God is waiting for our prayers to delight us. Leticia and Danny were expecting their second child. After a routine scan Leticia's heart sank. It showed half the cerebellum missing, the area of the brain that coordinates movement. The sky seemed to fall in. Hoping against hope, they asked all their friends and family to pray. "After many prayers," a second scan revealed that the cerebellum was present but obscured by a large tumor on the neck. The next week her husband, Danny, texted after an MRI, "I prayed more than ever in my life this week. The baby seems OK. It's most likely a (benign) cyst.

Also my mother-in-law rang today to say she is thinking of becoming Catholic." The baby was born healthy.

A few years after Jacob's death, Jill reflected:

After little Jacob died, I was in awe at the simplicity of our children's faith. It made me realize that children are born with a faith so pure and simple. They accept whatever they are told and continue life with a big smile.

In the weeks and months following, the children would occasionally break down sobbing, missing their brother. These were hard moments to watch and the pain inside was tremendous for all of us.

Again and again, we would tell our children not to waste this suffering. To use it very much to pray for the holy souls in purgatory. To offer up their sadness and know that in God's eyes nothing is every wasted.

We as parents have the ability to teach our children not to have a single care or worry in the world, as God's grace will always be adequate, yet with their simple faith they can learn to offer up so much from a young age.

We taught them how to turn their sadness into something supernatural and even to try and forget themselves and reach out to others in these moments. At times they would come home from school and tell me the most beautiful things . . . "Mum, today I felt sad but offered it up for . . ."

Their faith kept us going too.

We told them to always say "thank you, Jesus," because if Jesus gives you a suffering, it's because He loves you very much.

One day, my six-year-old daughter at the time, picked up a children's book she received from the funeral home. The book illustrated how we might feel the presence of our loved ones after they had passed away. I was hesitant to let her read it, as it mentioned that we might feel our brother or sister "in the wind" or "when we look at little animals." Upon glancing through, she said very matter-of-factly, "What rubbish. Jacob is in heaven with God!"

I had a good laugh!

Full of Love

The day had seemed like many others. The little girl jumped out of the car, ran inside, and kissed her father, saying, "Daddy, I love you." Then she ran out to help her mother unload the shopping, was hit by a car, and died in the arms of her parents. These last words to her father gave him much peace in his anguish. "This was God's way of showing me that my daughter was full of love when she died," he said. Her younger brother is now a parish priest, and her younger sister a doctor and a mother.

How important it is to finish well. And we will finish well to the extent that we live for others, to the extent that our hearts are full of love. As St. John Paul wrote,

> At the end of our life, we will be judged on love, on the acts of charity we have done to the "least" of our brothers and sisters (see Mt 25:31–45), but also on the courage and fidelity with which we have witnessed to Christ. In the Gospel he said: "So every one who acknowledges me before men, I also will acknowledge before my Father who is in heaven" (Mt 10:32–33).[11]

To be full of love at our death is to be a saint. The canonized saints are given to us as masterpieces to copy. The last words of many saints have been to speak of their

---

11. John Paul II, "Message of Pope John Paul II for World Migration Day, 1997" (August 21, 1996). Vatican website: https://www.vatican.va/content/john-paul-ii/en/messages/migration/documents/hf_jp-ii_mes_26081996_world-migration-day.html.

love. St. Therese finished her life saying, "My God, I love you."[12] Mother Teresa said, "Jesus I love you."[13] On their arrest, St. Edith Stein was heard to say to her sister, "Come, we are going for our people."[14] St. Faustina's final diary entry was:

> I am thoroughly enwrapped in God. My soul is being inflamed by His love. I only know that I love and am loved. That is enough for me. I am trying my best to be faithful throughout the day to the Holy Spirit and to fulfill His demands. I am trying my best for interior silence to be able to hear His voice.[15]

They offered their sufferings out of love. As Christ had the name of his Father on his lips at the moment of his death, some saints have had the name of Christ on their lips. Blessed Miguel Pro shouted to the firing

---

12. Philip Kosloski, "The last words of 11 saints before they died" (November 9, 2018). Aleteia website: https://aleteia.org/2018/11/09/the-last-words-of-11-saints-before-they-died/.

13. Philip Kosloski, "The last words of 11 saints before they died."

14. Vatican News Service, "Teresa Benedict of the Cross Edith Stein (1891-1942)." Vatican website: https://www.vatican.va/news_services/liturgy/saints/ns_lit_doc_19981011_edith_stein_en.html.

15. Maria Faustina Kowalska, *Diary of St. Faustina*, 1828. Seraphim website: www.seraphim.my/divinemercy/diary/text/Diary HC(1804-1828).htm.

squad, "Long live Christ the King!"[16] St. Joan of Arc, on the stake, repeated the name "Jesus, Jesus, Jesus."[17] Padre Pio said simply, "Jesus, Mary."[18] And St. Bernadette of Lourdes also turned to Mary: "Holy Mary, pray for me, a poor sinner."[19]

Beautiful Things

As a school student he had been irrepressible. He was the smallest player on the playground and made up for it with courage and heart. However, in late secondary school his world collapsed. His father was suffering mental illness and the family became destitute. And remarkably, in the midst of these trials his mother had become Catholic.

He meandered through his twenties in restless living. All his friends thought he had drifted from his faith, but his mother kept praying for him. At twenty-seven he passed away from cancer. It was a tough funeral.

---

16. RCL Benziger Saint's Resource website: http://saints resource.com/miguel-agustin-pro.

17. Philip Kosloski, "The last words of 11 saints before they died."

18. Philip Kosloski, "The last words of 11 saints before they died."

19. Theresa Aletheia Noble, "6 Saints' powerful dying words" (May 1, 2018). Aleteia website: https://aleteia.org/2018/05/01/6 -saints-powerful-dying-words/.

I remember the time and the place when his mother rang me several months after the funeral. Some phone calls are impossible to forget.

> I just wanted to tell you that they brought the boxes of his belongings from the apartment where he was when he passed away . . . and they contain beautiful things.
>
> There are books about our faith in which he was making notes in the margins, and there is a diary. Two weeks before he died, he wrote, "I just want to be holy, I want to die with a smile on my face."
>
> So now I know why, when they brought me to him after he had died, why he had the smile on his face.

It gets better in the end, and if it's still bad, it's not the end.

Anointing of the Sick

Model these convictions, attitudes, and actions, and talk about them to your child:

- Hope
- Trust

Ages for principal focus on these goals: seven years and upwards

Pray about these areas of example in your own life as a parent.

- Do I foster a great hope, leading my family to heaven where we will be united in eternity?
- Death is the doorway to heaven where Jesus awaits us. How do I react when I hear the news that someone has died?
- Do I model optimism? Do I model patience ("If it's still bad, it's not the end")?
- Do I offer up any negative feelings, turning them into a prayer of trust?
- Do I consider sometimes the privilege of giving my children example of a peaceful and trusting heart, even if our Lord should allow me a serious illness?
- Do I accept the will of God in my life, rectifying my first reactions whenever necessary?
- Do I respond to difficulties with prayer?
- Am I confident that God my Father, and my mother Mary, whom I have so often asked, "Pray for us now and at the hour of our death," will be with me in my last hours?

Education of head: Sow these convictions in your child.

- God my Father only sends me what is good for me, even if it is difficult.
- I thank God every day and ask his help to be good.
- I pray every day for those in need.
- I offer up things that are difficult, whether they are great or small.
- I pray for those relatives and friends who have passed away.

Education of heart: Education of a child's desires and feelings.

- I look forward to heaven.
- I accept difficulties and I trust that God will always give us what is best for us.
- The only great sadness is to be separated from God by unrepented sin.
- I like to visit those who are sick or even gravely ill. I can support them with my company and with my prayers.

CHAPTER 7

Holy Orders

Let everyone revere the deacons as Jesus Christ, the bishop as the image of the Father, and the presbyters as the senate of God and the assembly of the apostles. For without them one cannot speak of the Church.

–St. Ignatius of Antioch,
Letter to the Trallians
ca. AD 105

Priesthood is for few, but vocation is for all. For every single one of us God has written the book of our lives, a totally personalized script for us to follow, to live for others in this world, and to be marvelously happy in eternity. It is the privilege of parents to raise their children to seek out this book, to discover God's will for their lives.

The story of the medieval Queen Jadwiga shows what great good flows from putting God's plans in place of our own, and how this decision, even in marriage, brings about good over many generations. Jadwiga was, more than any other, responsible for the conversion of Lithuania, the last bastion of paganism in Europe, at the end of the fourteenth century. Jadwiga, eleven years old, was crowned queen of Poland in 1387. She had been raised with great love of God—it was her father who had enshrined the Black Madonna of Częstochowa. Although she was betrothed to a boy of whom she was very fond, her counselors advised her to accept the hand of the thirty-five-year-old pagan king of Lithuania who, if she married him, promised to become Catholic with all his people. She decided after prayer to put God's plans before her own, for the sake of the spread of the Christian faith.

Her husband kept his word, and within his lifetime all Lithuania became Catholic and the country remains 75 percent Catholic to this day. Jadwiga was an extraordinarily holy queen, interceding for peace between countries, helping the poor, attending daily Mass, and even bequeathing her jewels to the Jagellonian university. She died at twenty-five, after urging her husband to keep the countries united, which he did. St. John Paul prayed at her grave, beatified her in 1997, and appointed her as the patron of a united Europe.

In this section we not only consider the vocation to the priesthood, but also how parents may nurture in each child a desire to discover and follow the unique personal vocation to which he or she is called in the Church. This vocational sense arises most easily from understanding that God has a plan for each person and indicates to us how to discover that plan.

Honoring the Father

It was the last hours of a camp attended by about fifty fathers and their sons. I sought out the caretaker who had facilitated our stay at the Christian camp and said, "John, thank you, you are a wizard . . ." He cut me off emphatically: "No I'm not. I'm a son of the most high God." He clearly understood his relationship to God as his son. At the time it seemed an overreaction, but, in truth, our duty is to honor God our Father.

Consider the opening of the *Our Father*.

Our Father who art in heaven,
Hallowed be thy name,
Thy kingdom come,
Thy will be done on earth as it is in heaven.

There is a big lesson here we can easily miss: the totality of the first half of this prayer is focused on the honor that is due to the Father. Only in the second half do we present *our* wishes. This realization can lead to a radical readjustment in prayer priorities.

Remember, Jesus has given us this prayer. This is Jesus telling us that we should be preoccupied with the glory of the Father. We honor the Father by paying attention to him, uniting our hearts and minds to his will. We trust him, thank him, and offer ourselves. This is what love does.

Yet do we pray this way? Or is our focus on our needs and desire for forgiveness? Of course, it is good to make requests—"Whatever you ask in my name, I will do it," our Lord promises (Jn 14:13)—but we must never forget that the aim of our life must be the same as the aim of Jesus' life: to give glory to the Father. Jesus is our model: "I thank thee Father, Lord of heaven and earth" (Mt 11:25); "My food is to do the will of him who sent me" (Jn 4:34).

Look at Psalms 144–150. Like the finale of a fireworks show, the Book of Psalms ends in jubilant crescendo of praise of God. The hallelujahs of the last seven psalms lift the roof off. This is the way we are meant to pray.

And this is the task of every vocation: to lead us to the life that, in God's providence, he has best equipped us to give glory to God. Much depends on our being open to the vocation that God has prepared for us from all eternity.

Every Vocation Builds Up the Church

Chapter seventeen of St. John's Gospel is known as the "priestly prayer" of our Lord at the Last Supper. It is the treasured exemplar of Jesus' pouring his heart out in prayer to the Father. We want to know what fills his mind and heart at this terrible moment. Here are the first three verses.

Sacrament of Holy Orders

"The ministerial priesthood is a means by which Christ unceasingly builds up and leads his Church. For this reason it is transmitted by its own sacrament, the sacrament of Holy Orders."
Catechism of the Catholic Church, 1547

Priests of the Old Testament were anointed to offer sacrifices of atonement on behalf of the people. These priests were seen as mediators between God and men, and they were prefigurements of Christ himself, who, by restoring mankind to grace, is the only efficacious mediator.

At the Last Supper Jesus gave the apostles and their successors the power to share in his priesthood. "As thou didst send me into the world, so I have sent them into the world. And for their sake I consecrate myself, that they also may be consecrated in truth" (Jn 17:18–19). He specifically chose them, and empowered them to celebrate the Eucharist, to preach, and to forgive sins. Following Jesus' example, as the sacraments are instituted by Christ, the Church does not ordain women to the ministerial priesthood. Women, and in a foremost way Mary, are called to different, but also highly privileged, roles.

When Jesus had spoken these words, he lifted up his eyes to heaven and said, "Father, the hour has come; glorify thy Son that the Son may glorify thee, since thou hast given him power over all flesh, to give eternal life to all whom thou hast given him. And this is eternal life, that they know thee the only true God, and Jesus Christ whom thou hast sent."

In every line he is talking to the Father. Read the whole chapter through. There are two dominant impressions: Jesus' deep union with the Father, and his concern for the unity of those entrusted to him, including for us. On the night before his passion, he prays that we may be united, and that we be united with him. "[I pray] also for those who believe in me through their word, that they may all be one; even as thou, Father, art in me, and I in thee, that they also may be in us, so that the world may believe that thou hast sent me" (Jn 17:20–21).

It is the task of every Catholic to pray for and bring about this unity. Union with God and unity among ourselves are prerequisites for the Church. Disunity is death.

Jesus' words make clear that unity is a supernatural fruit, for which we must humbly pray. It is the Holy Spirit who builds up the Church and holds her in unity. As our souls are the principles of life and unity in our bodies, the Holy Spirit is the principle of life and unity of the Church. He is the architect and the builder. We are unskilled labor called to delight in the project and second his work.

Take this further: the Holy Spirit is the *soul* of the Church, and, as St. Paul teaches, the Church is the Mystical *Body* of Christ. St. Paul should know. When Jesus unceremoniously unhorsed Paul, and blinded him with the brightness of his face, Jesus asked, "Saul, Saul, why do you persecute me?" Jesus identifies himself with the Church. We are the Church.

This appreciation helps us understand why, in the Eucharistic prayers of the Mass, prayer for the Church features so prominently.

> . . . these holy and unblemished sacrifices, which we offer you firstly for your holy catholic Church. Be pleased to grant her peace, to guard, unite and govern her throughout the world, together with your servant Francis, our Pope . . .[1]

---

1. Eucharistic Prayer I, *The Roman Missal*, amended 3rd ed. (New York: International Commission on English in the Liturgy Corp., 2008), p. 633.

The Church is unutterably holy because she is the Body of Christ, but because we make up that body we must do all we can to keep her holy, knowing how woefully damaging in our sinfulness we can be. Our baptismal calling is to love and serve the Church. Our prayer must be Jesus' prayer. To be united with God is our mission in whatever path we take in life. God our Father, in his providence, places us in a specific environment, gives us talents and interests through which we can live out this calling, and invites our generous and free response.

The Liturgy of Ordination

Priestly ordination, by the New Testament practice of imposition of hands by a bishop, bestows an indelible sacramental character, or seal, making the one who is ordained a priest for life. The diaconate, the priesthood, and the episcopacy ("the fullness of the sacrament of Orders") are the three grades of the sacrament of holy orders.[2] Deacons are called to a ministry of service, preaching, celebrating baptisms and marriages, and officiating at

---

2. Second Vatican Council, Decree Concerning the Pastoral Office of Bishops in the Church *Christus Dominus* (October 28, 1965), 15. Vatican website: https://www.vatican.va/archive/hist_councils /ii_vatican_council/documents/vat-ii_decree_19651028_christus -dominus_en.html.

funerals. Priests are called to be shepherds of their flocks, celebrating the sacraments and preaching, all in union with their bishops. Bishops, in communion with the Pope, are called to leadership in the Church, and their first duty is that of teaching.

Ordination can only be performed by a bishop whose own episcopal ordination may be traced back to the apostles themselves. As ordination is pre-eminently a vocation, the bishop must invite candidates to ordination. Following the example of Christ, the Latin Church asks celibacy of the three grades of holy orders, with the exception of permanent deacons.

How Wise a Father

"Why did you want to become a priest?" one student asked Daniel, a former student at my school and then a seminarian, on a class visit. Daniel replied,

My father said to me when I was seven, "Daniel, why don't you pray every day to discover what God wants of you?" I did that, and then, when I was about twelve or thirteen, doing my thanksgiving after Mass in the school chapel, I felt an overwhelming sense of peace that I was meant to be a priest. And I have never doubted it since.

How wise was Daniel's father in talking to a young boy in this way? He did not say to his son "Pray to be a priest," but instead, "Pray to discover God's plan." God's plan is always best for us—the book is already written. Not only does God know from all eternity what he wants of each of us, but he has prepared the ground for our fruitfulness, if only we pray to discover his will. How easy it is, however, to impose our will rather than seek God's will. I had witnessed Daniel's prayer. He followed his father's advice.

Daniel was sent to Rome to finish his studies and be ordained to the diaconate. At Pope Francis' inauguration, Deacon Daniel brought the Fisherman's Ring to him on a pillow, and it was Deacon Daniel who sang the Prayers of the Faithful. A totally disproportionate gift; a remarkable sign. His father's advice was totally vindicated.

How reluctant we can be to see that God our Father has everything planned out. He knows what he wants of each of us and gives us the wherewithal to accomplish it. As Corrie ten Boom writes in her autobiographical *The Hiding Place* about her network to hide Dutch Jews during the Second World War, "This is what the past is for! Every experience God gives us, every person he puts in our lives, is the perfect preparation for the future that only He can see."[3] It was the same hard life of St. John Paul that prepared him. In the words of the tribute of Cardinal Andrzej Maria Deskur, "Everything the Holy Father endured in his life prepared him for what he had to be. Just as an arrow is ready for the shot from the bow. God prepares the proper people, he prepares his arrows."[4]

If Daniel's father had not taken seriously conversation with a small boy, if he had not had the faith and timing to put things as he did, if Daniel had not been taught to be generous with God, he perhaps would have missed this great invitation to loving friendship with God, this great condescension of our God. God our Father has planned for us a life project that will give us the greatest happiness, a personal and unique path of friendship with him and of service to others. We are invited to take up this invitation freely and with generous love. If we do our best, God does the rest. God knows how to make it all add up, but we need to do our best to write in the numbers.

When Fr. Daniel came back to the school to say Mass in the college chapel where he had first heard his calling,

---

3. Corrie ten Boom, *The Hiding Place* (London: Hodder and Stoughton, 1971), p. 6.

4. G. O'Connor, *The Universal Father: A Life of John Paul II*, (Bloomsburg Publishing, 2008), chap. 16, Kindle.

he again told the story of that moment in his thanks-giving, fifteen years before, when his vocation had been revealed to him. As he did so he pointed to the place where he had been sitting: "I was just there." The boy sitting there squirmed.

Answers in Prayer

The gift of a vocation reveals God's plan for our happiness from eternity. This is true of marriage and of wholly spiritual vocations also. God our Father is first of all a father, and will care for us and make our vocation clear to us, provided we don't put our fingers in our ears. And even if we are, for a time, distracted or preoccupied, he will reveal his plans for us. The only prerequisite is that we pray seriously: "Ask, and it will be given you" (Mt 7:7). This is true for every vocation, including marriage. It would be totally foolish to found the direction of our life on anything except God's will.

A vocation is the path God gives us along which we will learn to love him above all things, to turn our lives into love. Every vocation from God is meant to lead us to this purity of heart. It is our personal path to holiness, to see God. Vocation is not a signed contract in the mail; we trust not in a piece of paper but in the light God sends us in prayer, knowing that he has told us, "Knock and [the door] will be opened to you" (Mt 7:7). We make our decision in the presence of God according to our best lights, and God will always back us. This is true for spiritual vocations and for marriage.

Sometimes God goes to extraordinary lengths to make a vocation clear. In the case of Greg, the idea of this vocation started when three different people he did not know told him he would make a good priest. After the third encounter, he began to wonder himself. Greg, the school vice-captain, announced at the school valedictory dinner that he had been accepted into the seminary. We stood and applauded. It was an unforgettable moment. Fr. Greg went on to do his theological doctorate in Oxford.

In the weeks prior to his ordination, I met up with Greg for coffee. We were speaking about ways to support ex-students of the college. I wanted his suggestions too on how we could improve the religion classes. Greg spoke passionately about the need to make religion "doable and attractive." He believed the effectiveness of parenting is proportionate to the humility of the parent. "The humility of parents is so attractive to children," he explained.

"It's the natural goodness that attracts. We must encourage parents to be trusting . . . not watching and checking."

Another graduate, Chris, had captained the school's basketball team to victory in the intercollege finals by sinking a three-pointer just as the clock ran out. He spoke glowingly about the faith of his parents and their commitment to the Rosary each night. He spoke of his remarkable discovery of his calling.

> The moment of elevation of the consecrated host at World Youth Day changed my life. I was profoundly moved by my unworthiness. Later that day, at 11 PM, I was praying in the chapel where we were staying. My prayer was a two-hour rant, with tears and the works. A priest came in, saw my distress, and said to me, "God makes worthy the unworthy. Dive into God's love and follow his will."

A third example: One evening, a nine-year-old boy named Epeli was saying the Rosary with his cousins in a village hut in the Fijian mountains. A cousin said simply to him, "You would make a good priest." It never left him. There was one unforgettable evening in a teachers' college when he walked along the shore and asked God to grant him a period of time to teach after which he would enter the seminary. Later we sponsored him to Australia, he taught with us for the four years his visa allowed, and then he was accepted into the Sydney seminary. He is now vocations director in the Archdiocese of Sydney.

Nevertheless, we should not think that our specific calling, even though it comes from God and is his will for us, will always be accompanied by an extraordinary light. The Second Vatican Council says that the vocation to the priesthood does not require extraordinary manifestations but comes to us "in the manner in which the will of God is daily made known to prudent Christians."[5] In other words, we may not be thrown off our horse when we discover our vocation, nor may it be accompanied even by an extraordinary peace of heart that can sometimes be present, but it will be present in prayer, in good advice, and in looking calmly in the presence of God at the talents and aspirations that God has formed in us.

---

5. Second Vatican Council, Decree on the Ministry and Life of Priests *Presbyterorum Ordinis* (December 7, 1965), 11. Vatican website: https://www.vatican.va/archive/hist_councils/ii_vatican_council/documents/vat-ii_decree_19651207_presbyterorum-ordinis_en.html.

Life Is for Giving

Almost fifty years ago, as a young priest, Fr. Jerry Gehringer came to Australia from the American Midwest. Through these decades he has been an extraordinarily effective school chaplain and advisor to young adults. He likes to remind young people, "When I was a boy, we would often hear 'Life is for giving,' but we don't say that now."

Pope Francis warns us of our culture of "extreme individualism."[6] We live in an increasingly self-centered society, and as a consequence it is all too easy to overlook the fundamental truth that life is about giving of ourselves. We dismiss the words of our Lord, "It is more blessed to give than to receive" (Acts 20:35). The essence of every vocational response is to give of ourselves, freely and lovingly. This is true for the priesthood, but also for marriage and every spiritual pathway that God presents to man.

---

6. Francis, Apostolic Exhortation *Amoris Laetitia* (March 19, 2016), 33. Vatican website: https://www.vatican.va/content /francesco/en/apost_exhortations/documents/papa-francesco _esortazione-ap_20160319_amoris-laetitia.html.

We can have the mistaken idea that a vocation is something static, that we passively receive it and that nothing we do can alter that dynamic. But the teaching of the Church is that God also gives us a part in bringing all this about. He counts on our free and generous desires. St. John Paul describes vocation as a "dialogue . . . between the love of God who calls and the freedom of individuals who respond lovingly to him."[7]

God listens to us. "God takes the initiative but is respectful of the freedom that makes it decisive," St. Paul VI explains.[8] This can also be true of the vocational path we are called to discover in life. God has given us certain talents and the wherewithal to put those talents at his service, but he also invites us to do this totally freely and with love. He invites us to "want" the vocation to which he is calling us. Just as a young couple fulfill both their own desires *and* the will of God in heaven

---

7. John Paul II, Post-Synodal Apostolic Exhortation *Pastores Dabo Vobis* (March 25, 1992), 36. Vatican website: https://www .vatican.va/content/john-paul-ii/en/apost_exhortations/documents /hf_jp-ii_exh_25031992_pastores-dabo-vobis.html.

8. Paul VI, Homily "Solenne Concelebrazione per le Vocazioni" (April 20, 1975). Vatican website: https://www.vatican.va/content /paul-vi/it/homilies/1975/documents/hf_p-vi_hom_19750420 .html. [Translation ours.]

when each says "I do" at the altar, God invites us all to seek out, identify, and throw ourselves into the path that we believe he has prepared us for, even if that path will have some slippery rocks and precipices. He is holding our hand.

A vocation to marriage, to priesthood or religious life, or apostolic single life, is a free invitation to the path of greatest happiness mapped out for us from all eternity. By baptism we are already friends of Jesus. He cares deeply for us and accompanies us in difficult decisions.

And God is such a faithful friend, that even if we say no to the path of greatest happiness he has planned for us, of course he continues to help us. Pope Benedict writes emphatically, that if I reject God's specific call with a no, he does not write me off but "opens up a new path of love"[9] for me. He is a loyal friend even when I am not. The danger is that we harden our hearts to his plans, and no matter how many opportunities he gives us, no matter how many paths he opens, we still insist on walking off the track.

---

9. Benedict XVI, *Jesus of Nazareth, vol. 2, Holy Week: From the Entrance into Jerusalem to the Resurrection* (San Francisco: Ignatius Press, 2011), p. 120.

Uncommon Sacrifice

Sacrifices are for all of us. The priest stared at the trembling handgun that was pointing at him. He offered a cigarette to calm the gunman, saying, "Here this will help you relax." "No thanks, Father, it's Lent," he replied. At least the nervous robber did understand one thing well about our faith.[10]

People of all times have understood intuitively that we offer the things we value to the one we love. Every sacrifice should be a gesture of love. And when we fail to do this, the sacrifice is worthless. Consider Cain who did not offer to God the best he had; or even the diabolically distorted human sacrifice of the Aztecs.

Sacrifice however must be offered by someone with standing in the eyes of the one to whom it is offered. The Jews had their high priests who offered immolated bullocks and sheep, and Jesus Christ, the eternal high priest, offers himself. In his divinity and sonship, Jesus has standing with God and, in his humanity, he can represent us.

---

10. This was a joke told by Fr. Ramon Dodero which may have foundation in truth.

Calvary is the supreme sacrifice from which all other offerings draw value. The ministerial priest participates in the priesthood of Christ. The spiritual writer Romano Guardini points out that the minister speaks, as God, the words of consecration with the same creative force of the words that brought the universe into existence.[11]

When we are baptized and in grace, we are in Christ. So we all share in the priesthood of Christ, the "common priesthood." And this means that we can offer sacrifices that are in union with the sacrifice of our Lord. *Lumen Gentium*, Vatican II's Constitution of the Church, describes the baptized as a people who,

> by regeneration and the anointing of the Holy Spirit, are consecrated as a spiritual house and a holy priesthood, in order that through all those works which are those of the Christian man they may offer spiritual sacrifices and proclaim the power of Him who has called them out of darkness into His marvelous light (cf. 1 Pt 2:4–10).[12]

---

11. Romano Guardini, *Preparing Yourself for Mass* (Manchester, NH: Sophia Institute Press, 1997), pp. 76-82.

12. *Lumen Gentium*, 10.

By virtue of our baptism, and therefore united with Christ, we are able to offer sacrifices that honor him, thank him, atone for sin, and intercede for others. This is big. But let's also remember that the worth of our lives is measured by love, and sacrifices must be an offering of love or they simply don't count. So many other surprising, good things come from a spirit of sacrifice. The Curé of Ars said simply, "The cross is a gift of God to his friends."[13]

Called to Courage

"Who is worthy to celebrate Mass? To hold Christ in his hands?" proclaimed Fr. Walter Macken in a personal conversation and with impressive humility. Because the task of celebrating Mass is so lofty, the priest must strive to be especially prayerful and close to God. Notwithstanding the truly awful accounts of clerical (and nonclerical) abuse, the Church has never lacked holy priests. In every age, there have been priests moved by the Holy Spirit to give of themselves unstintingly. Look too at the

---

13. Alfred Monnin, *Life of the Curé D'Ars* (Baltimore: Kelly & Piet, 1865), p. 146.

heroic efforts of so many clergy in Europe during the Black Death. In the space of four years, 1347 to 1351, 31 percent of the population of Europe is estimated to have died, but for Catholic clergy the figure was close to 50 percent, as they lay down their own lives to minister to the dying.[14]

This readiness to give of one's life is well demonstrated in the lives of missionaries and martyrs. The average life expectancy of a nineteenth-century missionary was five and a half years, due to exhausting and health-sapping work. Consider too the prospects of the sixteenth-century priests who would steal back into England during the reign of Queen Elizabeth I to minister to persecuted Catholics, only to be hanged, drawn, and quartered.

St. Peter Chanel, patron of Oceania, worked—seemingly without spiritual fruit—on the island of Fortuna and was then brutally murdered at the age of thirty-seven. Yet after his death, in a short period of time most of the island converted, including his murderer, Musumusu, who asked to be buried outside the church

---

14. Warren H. Carroll, *The Glory of Christendom* (Front Royal, VA: Christendom Press, 1993), p. 394.

at Poi so that pilgrims coming to pray to Peter Chanel would walk over his grave.

The recent history of the Church in Communist China has been marked by great suffering, even in the most recent years according to a US Congressional hearing.[15] All mainland Chinese under the age of 18 may not attend Church or receive religious instruction at risk of heavy penalties.[16] The new crackdown on Christians and the Catholic Church is the worst since the murders perpetrated during the Cultural Revolution under the Maoist slogan, "Eradicate Religion."[17] News service Zenit documents the 2020 arrest of dozens of priests and a number of bishops. Other bishops remain missing after

---

15. The Communist Party's crackdown on religion in China; hearing before the Congressional-Executive Commission on China, 115th Congress, second session (Washington, D.C.: US Government Publishing Office, 2019). Available at: https://www.govinfo.gov /content/pkg/CHRG-115hhrg33238/html/CHRG-115hhrg33238.htm

16. Gerard O'Connell, "Pope Francis to Chinese Catholics: The church is praying for you 'in the midst of difficulties'" (May 23, 2018). America Magazine - The Jesuit Review website: https:// www.americamagazine.org/faith/2018/05/23/pope-francis-chinese -catholics--church-praying-you-midst-difficulties.

17. Anthony E. Clark, "China's Modern Martyrs: From Mao to Now (Part 3)" (March 25, 2014). The Catholic World Report website: https://www.catholicworldreport.com/2014/03/25/chinas-modern -martyrs-from-mao-to-now-part-3/.

arrest decades ago. Once again, church property is being burned, and churches blown up or demolished.[18] Let us hold priests in preeminent respect because of the great dignity bestowed on them in bringing Christ to us in the Eucharist and in bringing us to Christ in all the sacraments, and because they are called in a particular way, as true Christs, to lay down their lives. And this remains true despite the crisis of the priesthood in Australia and in many western countries: increasing average age, reduced numbers of parishioners, amalgamated parishes, and saddest of all (even though it involves a very low percentage of priests), the tragic reality of sexual abuse of minors.

The Old Testament tells the story of Moses' victory in the Battle of Rephidim over the Amalekites. Moses prayed with his hands upraised. "Aaron and Hur held up his hands, one on one side, and the other on the other side" (Ex 17:12).[19] As long as Moses kept up his hands in

---

18. Zenit, "Persecution of Catholics in China" (2000). CERC website: https://www.catholiceducation.org/en/controversy/persecution/persecution-of-catholics-in-china.html.

19. Hur is a further bridge in this story between these ancient events and the new covenant of the Messiah: the Book of Chronicles (1 Chron 4:4) tells us he was the founder of Bethlehem, "house of

prayer, the battle was successful. What is our takeaway from this? Difficulties are meant to make us pray, but prayer is infallibly successful, albeit at times in ways we did not envision. Moses' arms were supported by the priest Aaron—for us this means that we should rely on the Mass. What great power Jesus gives us, and most especially to priests. Do you and I recognize the great condescension of God to place such power in the hands of men?

Holy Orders
Model these convictions, attitudes, and actions, and talk about them to your child: • Magnanimity   • Trust
Ages for principal focus on these goals: Seven years and upwards

---

bread." Note that 1 Chron 2:51 and 54 suggests his son to be the founder. Also note discussion in Richard Buckham *Gospel Women: Studies in the named women of the Gospels* (Grand Rapids, MI: Wm B. Eerdmans Publishing, 2002), p. 38.

Pray about these areas of example in your own life as a parent.

- Am I determined to spend my life living out God's will for me, to the very best of my ability?
- Do I often say prayers that glorify God? For example, "Glory be to the Father . . ."
- Do I see my vocation to marriage as service to the Church?
- Do I model generosity in every aspect of my life, that life is "for giving" and this is where holiness lies?
- Through the common priesthood, do I intercede for others, as another Christ, by my prayer and sacrifices?
- Do I only speak well of all priests and bishops, keeping them in my prayers?
- Do I seek advice for my life in regular spiritual direction?

Education of head: Sow these convictions in your child.

- Everything God my Father sends me is for my happiness and holiness.
- God our Father has a plan for my life, an invitation to holiness and special friendship. In prayer I discover that plan.
- My vocation will always be a vocation to live for others in some way.

Education of heart: Education of a child's desires and feelings.

- I am very grateful to God for having a plan for my life that will lead me to holiness and happiness. I ask him to show it to me.
- I practice generosity daily in small deeds.
- Helping my parents and others makes me happy.
- Obeying the will of God and my parents should make me happy.

CHAPTER 8

Matrimony

There is nothing better in this world than that husband and wife be of one mind.

–HOMER
CA. 800 BC[1]

A former Baptist, now Catholic, and a US Marine, Tim Staples had just finished a talk to parents and young adults on Adam and Eve and God's plan for marriage. A young man put up his hand and asked the first question. "Mr. Staples, thank you for that wonderful talk.

---

1. Homer, *The Odyssey*, 6:180-185.

My name is Gerry. There are my parents over there. I just want to be like my parents. I just want to get married. How do I meet the girl of my dreams?"

Tim spoke of how, after his conversion, he met his own wife in a providential encounter at a church activity. Then he said, "Understand that Jesus wants you to meet the woman of your dreams more than you do. Pray every day to meet her."[2]

Marriage is a gift of God to humanity. It is a school where the students learn of their own great calling to live for others. In this classroom they discover the mission that God has planned for them from all eternity, and they are invited to discover the privilege of being loved exclusively by another. Commitments of responsibility to others, and knowing that we are worthy of such reciprocal love of another, deliver human maturity.

But we must never forget that the largest role is played by the grace of the sacrament itself. So prepare your children so that marriage is not a walk down the aisle on one so-beautiful day, but that it is instead day after day for one's whole life, drawing strength from this great sacrament.

---

2. Personal anecdone of the words of Tim Staples in a talk to parents and ex-students at Redfield College, Sydney, 2008.

God's Plan for Happiness and Holiness

Viktor Frankl, who was introduced earlier, writes of the power of love to deliver maturity, to change us for the better. Both at the human and the spiritual level love gives us strength to change and to do good. He argues that love helps the beloved become as the lover sees him or her. For the loved one wants to be worthy of the lover, a worthier recipient of love, by growing to be more like the lover's image, and so he becomes more and more the image of "what God conceived and wanted him to be."[3]

Love puts the other person first. Time tested advice to maintain unity comes from Mr. and Mrs. Percy Arrowsmith, who for a time held the *Guinness Book of Records* longest marriage entry of over eighty years. When asked for their secret, Mrs. Arrowsmith thought carefully and replied, "Never go to bed without making up." But Percy didn't have to think as long: "Always say, 'Yes, dear!'"[4]

---

3. Viktor E. Frankl, *The Doctor and the Soul: An Introduction to Logotherapy* (New York: Knopf, 1955), p. 150.

4. Steven Morris, "80-year wedlock a world record," *The Guardian*, June 1, 2005, www.theguardian.com/uk/2005/jun/01 /stevenmorris.

In any case, let us try not to be like the husband who walked behind his wife who was struggling in with packages from the car. With some difficulty the back door was negotiated and the load deposited in the kitchen. To her exasperated question, "Why didn't you help me?" he responded, "You looked like you were coping."

The Liturgy of Matrimony

For the sacrament to be valid, a man and woman must express their irrevocable free choice to give themselves exclusively to each other and to receive the gift of their spouse. The marriage is contracted before the local bishop or pastor, or before a priest or deacon delegated by either of them, in front of two witnesses. Within Mass in a church is the most appropriate setting.

Dietrich von Hildebrand stresses that sacramental marriage is of an infinitely higher order than natural marriage; it becomes a state that is holy in itself, and which sanctifies the spouses.

"The act of voluntary surrender of one's own person to another with the intention of forming a permanent and intimate union of love, creates an objective bond which, once established, is withdrawn from the sphere of arbitrary decision of the persons concerned. . . . This solemn act of marriage attains further an infinitely higher importance and

> power if it is consciously fulfilled in Christ and if it contains in a way a consecration of both partners to Christ."[5]

And what of the heroic self-giving of the parents of big families? Rosa Pich, one of sixteen, is herself the mother of eighteen. Four months after she lost her husband to aggressive cancer, up she gets to lead her children, the youngest still only seven, along the Camino of Saint James in a six-week expedition. She writes simply:

> Children make you look outside and think more about others and less about yourself. They help you to pass over the earthly banalities, among other reasons, because you have little time to look at yourself in the mirror and contemplate yourself.[6]

Some people are simply extraordinary.

How impressive to read that St. Catherine of Siena was the twenty-third of twenty-four children. We know

---

5. Dietrich von Hildebrand, *Marriage: The Mystery of Faithful Love* (Manchester, NH: Sophia Institute Press, 1997), p. 23.
6. Rosa Pich, *Rosa, What's Your Secret? Raising a Large Family with Love* (New York: Scepter, 2016).

much about her father's kindness, and that her mother became her daughter's most loyal supporter and advocate, but what generosity! What amazing faith and what an amazing gift they have given to the world.

God's Plan for Sex

In the contemporary climate how difficult it is to raise children who are pure—or even to keep ourselves pure. Purity is neither prudery nor sexual repression. It is not a negative in the least. Paul Ricoeur, the great contemporary French philosopher, insists that sex and commitment cannot be separated, and when they are, there is a great price to pay: "Everything that makes the sexual encounter free speeds its collapse into insignificance."[7] Sex becomes mere entertainment. Family is disposable.

Dietrich von Hildebrand's philosophy provided the foundation for St. John Paul's Theology of the Body. "Sex necessarily involves a revelation of the deepest personal intimacy,"[8] von Hildebrand observed, and "to make the

---

7. As quoted in Josef Pieper, *Faith, Hope, Love* (San Francisco: Ignatius Press, 1997).

8. Dietrich von Hildebrand, *In Defense of Purity* (Steubenville: Hildebrand Press, 2017), p. 2.

sexual surrender is to anchor oneself most firmly to the world and to enter into the closest union with one's fellow creatures."[9] And so he wrote of the "fearful profanation"[10] involved when sexual pleasure becomes an end itself, or is pursued outside of the divine plan of marriage. Such impurity is degrading for the person involved; desecrating, in that it is a misuse of God's gift; and defiling, because it separates us from God in our being.

The very nature of sex is that it creates a permanent bond between persons, "a tie of such infinite tenderness and such deep proximity, so essentially *permanent*, implying such a radical surrender, that it cannot be repeated with another person as long as the person is alive to whom one has given oneself."[11] And therefore, he says, sex outside marriage is a "degradation and desecration of the union destined as the ultimate realization of the communion of love."[12]

It is important to explain to your teenager that when a man and woman allow themselves to become

---

9. von Hildebrand, *In Defense of Purity*, p. 50.

10. von Hildebrand, *In Defense of Purity*, p. 39.

11. Dietrich von Hildebrand, *Marriage: The Mystery of Faithful Love* (Nashua, NH: Sophia Institute Press, 1984), p. 25.

12. von Hildebrand, *In Defense of Purity*, p. 29.

sexually intimate they trigger the brain chemistry and pathways meant to underpin permanent commitments and stable families. Because if they do fall into sexual activity before they have reached a decision about marriage, or about their partner for life, they have already hormonally and psychologically bonded themselves to each other. Thus, to some degree a free decision has been taken out of their hands.

Von Hildebrand argued that monogamy alone is not enough. God must be a witness. He insisted that if a couple do not accept, as it were, the divine blueprint for human sexual behavior, their love for each other will degenerate into a love of self. They will almost inevitably pursue sex for self-centered reasons. By divine design, human beings will only be fulfilled in sexual relationships if the husband and wife care deeply and exclusively for each other and are not interfering with the natural life-giving potential of their sexual relationship.[13]

---

13. The higher incidence of divorce evident in users of artificial contraception appears to support this view: see Mercedes Arzu Wilson, "The Practice of Natural Family Planning Versus the Use of Artificial Birth Control: Family, Sexual and Moral issues," *Catholic Social Science Review* 7 (2002), pp. 185–211; Walter Rhomberg, Michaela Rhomberg, and Hubert Weissenbach H., "Natural Family Planning as a Family Binding Tool: A Survey Report," *Catholic*

The purposes of marriage are, to use the memorable words of theologian and author Janet Smith, "babies and bonding."[14] By this she means, in addition to indissolubility, that sexual intimacy must be open to life. To avoid fertility without a good reason betrays a self-seeking that contradicts the "radical surrender" of marriage. Marriage, if lived as God intended, *must* lead to holiness.

Holy Realism

In the encyclical *Amoris Laetitia*, Pope Francis offers an unusual observation: "Love coexists with imperfection."[15] No one is immune to failure concerning the obligations of husbands and wives. We are all *vulnerable*—from the Latin word for wounded. Our wounds are our poor self-control that leads to self-indulgent, impulsive actions. We excuse self-serving rationalizations for those failings,

---

Social Science Review 18 (2013), pp. 63–70; and Richard J. Fehring, "Under the Microscope: The Influence of Ever Use of Natural Family Planning and Contraceptive Methods on Divorce Rates as Found in the 2006–2010 National Survey of Family Growth," *Current Medical Research* 24, nos. 3 and 4 (Summer/Fall 2013), pp. 12–16.

14. Janet Smith, "Humanae Vitae, Cracking the Contraceptive Myths," YouTube video, posted by North Texas Catholic, April 28, 2018, www.youtube.com/watch?v=3yBPmQDF5iI.

15. *Amoris Laetitia*, 113.

turning them quickly into vices. These human failings play havoc in marriages when partners fail to invest in each other, focus on negatives in each other, and allow other substitutes in their hearts such as overwork, sports, or an old friend or work colleague, which then quickly fill up a shrunken heart. Reasons and reality fail to correct our imbalance when we surrender to emotional responses. This is resolved not by a change of mind, but of heart.

A much publicized study by Professor Arthur Aron and colleagues demonstrated that in a significant number of cases merely a discussion of personal opinions and staring into the eyes of someone of the opposite sex can initiate romantic attachments.[16] If that is the case, then when arguments, trips away, or lack of time together weakens our bonds at home, all too easily our personal assistant or colleague in a work team can become surprisingly attractive.

Vital life skills that children need are the capacities to apologize and to forgive. Remember that King David

---

16. Arthur Aron et al., "The Experimental Generation of Interpersonal Closeness: A Procedure and Some Preliminary Findings," *Personality and Social Psychology Bulletin* 23, no. 4 (April 1997), pp. 363–377, https://www.stafforini.com/docs/Aron%20et%20al%20%20The%20experimental%20generation%20of%20interpersonal%20closeness.pdf.

not only stole the wife of one of his soldiers, but that he orchestrated that loyal man's death to cover his perversion. It was a terrible sin, but, coming to his senses, he repented and humbly accepted the consequences of his actions, which included the death of his illicitly conceived infant as well as rebellion and the death of his son Absalom. In old age, his pride led him to folly, delighting in the armed strength of his kingdom. Once again, truly contrite, he accepted punishment with trust in God, and now he is revered as a great saint. Great sins are no obstacle to great holiness, provided we have the humility to acknowledge them and make good as best we can.

Show It, Don't Just Say It

Faithfulness, on the other hand, builds on itself. The graces of the sacrament of matrimony give couples all the help they need to sanctify their state, to become holy in their duties as spouse and parent, and to keep up their hope. The money is in the bank, but we need to draw it out. We make withdrawals by heartfelt prayer and by personal effort to be the best we can be.

Change yourself; don't seek to change your spouse. Let grace and example do their work. The backstory to

Arthur Miller's *The Crucible* is that the flawed hero, John Proctor, was unfaithful to Elizabeth, his wife. She took the fault on herself, heartfeltly acknowledging, "It needs a cold wife to prompt lechery." Proctor, too, admitted his guilt and took full responsibility. Of course he was the one who cheated, but beneath the action is a deep truth about human beings: that we all carry imperfections and these have the potential to be our undoing.

Pope Benedict has spoken of the clear link between the crisis in faith and the crisis in marriage.[17] This means, if couples are to make a great success of their marriage and family life, they need to have a strong faith. There are many obstacles to be overcome, both in our own personalities and in the world in which we walk. Faith fortifies us.

Remember the gospel scene where the apostles are ferrying Jesus across the Sea of Galilee when a storm strikes them? The boat is taking water and the fishermen, in their experience, fear the worst. They wake Jesus. He stills the storm with a word, and asks, "Why are you

---

17. Benedict XVI, Speech "Address of his Holiness Benedict XVI for the Inauguration of the Judicial Year of the Tribunal of the Roman Rota" (January 26, 2013). Vatican website: https://www.vatican .va/content/benedict-xvi/en/speeches/2013/january/documents /hf_ben-xvi_spe_20130126_rota-romana.html.

afraid? Have you no faith?" (Mk 4:40) Faith drives out fear. The fear in marriages and family is of a different type, but nevertheless just as paralyzing. It is a fear of losing love, a fear of wasting our life and potential, a fear of not connecting with our husband or teenager, a fear of all the challenges of balancing budget, feeding an extra child, late nights, and no space for ourselves. If we live by faith, we do not fear.

A ten-year-old was riding home after school with his father, on Valentine's Day. "Dad, are you stopping to get Mom some flowers?" he asked. Dad huffed back, "I don't believe in all that commercial nonsense."

"Dad, it's not what you believe, it's what Mom likes!" The boy is made of the same blunt honesty as the father. Dad listened, stopped, bought the flowers, had a wonderful night, and with humility told his work colleagues the story the next day.

Love in theory is not love. The languages of love must be practiced. Either a commitment of love is shown in concrete actions or it does not exist. Without hesitation, Pat, who has worked for three decades in Catholic marriage education, nominates a sure-fire tip to help couples: "small acts of kindness." Show your love. Whether it is in small details, finding the right love language, or loving your spouse the way he or she wants to be loved, the key message is the same. Make it real.

One young woman has discovered the power of physical touch. "My husband speaks in bullet points when he is tired: 'How was work?' 'Same as yesterday.' Yet he feels rejected if I don't touch him." She uses this love language to reach her husband. "And I strive to keep eye contact. He can tell when I'm mad because I never keep eye contact."

Sadly, one lawyer observes, "Men are three years behind what their wives are thinking." This can be catastrophic when there is a lack of open and frank communication that is without blame and emotional charge. One woman may exhort, "Wives *tell* your husband what you want, he will *never* read your mind." And a husband may say: "Tell your wife what you want to say, don't assume a message is communicated."

Fully Present

Even if she is just clever, computer code Siri can teach us something about the importance of respect. On calling Siri a name that polite persons never use, even to a machine, she replied with a grandmotherly, "Now, Now!"

The second time, she curtly replied, "I respect you." But it is the scene of the Annunciation which truly captures the meaning of respect. Gabriel did not tell Mary what to do but invited her cooperation, leaving her totally free.

Hand-in-hand with respect for freedom, stress the positive. Case in point: Parents with a hard-to-handle daughter, about fourteen, and a list of problems. The couple agreed not to rise from the table until their list of her good qualities was at least as long. Her mother summed up: "This simple exercise was a game-changer. When we do not seek things to admire in each person around us, we easily become fixated on the negatives."

Plato offered a sobering view of all this: "He who is corrupted does not easily appreciate the beauty of others."[18] Or in more positive terms, we must seek to imitate God, who loves us first. If we love others first, we can bring them with us. Mother Teresa said as much to one of her helpers who was having difficulty gaining the cooperation of an old man in her homes: "If you loved him more, you would be able to feed him."[19]

---

18. Plato, *Phaedrus*, 249D-251A.
19. Personal anecdote, as related by Fr. Dominique Faure, address at Theology at the Pub, May 2018, Melbourne.

The bottom line is that our Lord's new commandment, "Love one another as I have loved you," is first and foremost to be lived out in these gardens of love that are our families. And to lead the way is wholly your responsibility as a parent, not your child's.

Marriage educator Emerson Eggerichs draws attention to the profound respect present in a loving relationship.[20] When respect departs, love dies. It is an ongoing readiness to honor each other, to give importance to what they think and say, to pay attention, to notice. Consider the practical wisdom of Pope Francis in *Amoris Laetitia*:

- We can be fully present to others only by giving fully of ourselves and forgetting all else. Our loved ones merit our complete attention.
- Those who love not only refrain from speaking too much about themselves but are focused on others; they make them the center of attention.
- Take time—quality time. Listen patiently and attentively. It requires the self-discipline of not speaking until the time is right.

---

20. Emerson Eggerichs, *Love and Respect for a Lifetime* (Nashville: Thomas Nelson, 2010).

- Use three words: Please. Thanks. Sorry. Three essential words! [21]

Reading biographies of great men and women in happy marriages helps us see that success in relationships is also a function of character and can inspire us in the face of so many stories in our time of marriage breakup and conflict. For example, Aristotle was universally regarded as a kind and affectionate man. In his will he wrote of his happy family life and made generous provision for Herpyllis to whom he was devoted after his wife died. He praised the "constant love she has shown me." He also provided with solicitous care for his children and servants. It is no surprise that this wonderful man wished to leave to his son, as a precious legacy, guidelines for a happy and virtuous life in the *Nicomachean Ethics*.

So too, Anna Dostoyevskaya wrote of her marvelous marriage with the great Russian author,

> Throughout my life it has always seemed a kind of mystery to me that my good husband not only loved and respected me as many husbands love and respect

---

21. *Amoris Laetitia*, 133–141.

their wives, but almost worshipped me, as though I were some special being created just for him.[22]

True love may or may not come with a spontaneous emotional surge, but it will always pass this respect test, in both directions.

Supernatural Resources

All had seemed harmonious. Their youngest daughter had just graduated from school—mission accomplished—the last of the couple's three children to graduate. Then one day, all they had worked hard to accomplish together came crashing down. The husband, an insurance middle manager, arrived home one night to his wife who announced, "I have to get a life. I'm moving out." The husband was devastated, however, from the first devastating moment, had the humility to recognize that he had contributed to this situation. He assured his wife he would do all he could to help her, ensuring she had access to their money on a joint account—their entire assets.

---

22. Anna Dostoyevskaya, *Dostoevsky: Reminiscences* (New York: Liveright, 1975).

As the situation dragged on, she asked for settlement of the property. He was more than equitable, continuously assuring her that he realized he had not cared for her well and that he would be there for her if and when she wished to come back. Ironically, the company which he had served very well had made him redundant. With more time suddenly on his hands, he changed his life by going to daily Mass and rekindling a deep devotion to Our Lady. He found a spiritual director who gave him ongoing support. He went to Lourdes on a pilgrimage and prayed for his wife, children, and marriage.

After three years, his wife requested a divorce. After four, she moved out of state. At the start of the fifth year, he confided to a friend, "I have been told in prayer that it will get worse, but then it will be better. We will be together again and be an example for others." Sure enough, things got worse. His former wife went on an overseas holiday with her new boyfriend.

The sixth year after their split, the two sat together in their home speaking about the miraculous recovery of their marriage. The wife said, "The man I dated was lying about, feeling unwell. I was paddling on the lagoon, and suddenly I felt a voice deep within me saying, 'Go back to the arms of the one who loves you.'" She was in no doubt that Our Lord had spoken to her heart. "You don't ignore a voice like that," she told her husband. "I came back to Sydney and called you and said, 'I want to come home.' You said to me, 'Come home.'"

They renewed their wedding vows and travelled back to the country where they were born. There, they inexplicably found themselves on national television talking about how they got their marriage back. "Our Blessed Mother changes hearts, and don't I know it," was the wife's testimony.

Let us never forget that matrimony is a sacrament bringing the supernatural resources to heal, provided we do not give up hope.

Hearts and Minds

A core message throughout this book has been that your family is a school where both parents and children learn to live for others. St. John Paul said that it is from this selflessness of parents that children develop an understanding of God's love: "Their parental love is called to become for the children the visible sign of the very love of God."[23] This is a high calling, empowered by the grace

_____

23. John Paul II, Apostolic Exhortation *Familiaris Consortio* (November 22, 1981), 14. Vatican website: https://www.vatican.va

of the sacrament of matrimony. Consider the maturity of the young man in the following story and how much it tells us about the way his parents have raised him.

One afternoon after school, a young law student wandered into bookshop where a book launch was about to begin. He happily helped himself to the finger food and decided to sit in. It turned out that the main speaker was a prominent judge and the book was a study of LGBT sociology. Unknowingly, he had crashed a gay book launch. The judge criticized a skewed interpretation of Catholic sexual teaching. Undeterred, the young man put up his hand and said directly, "I feel you have misrepresented the position of the Catholic Church on sex." The judge rebuffed him, but the student held his ground and a lively debate followed.

Later, the impressed judge approached him and gave him his business card.

A measure of the effectiveness of your parenting will be whether your child has adopted your deepest values and whether he or she will be faithful in love. It is a question of explicit preparation as well as example. Pope Benedict

---

/content/john-paul-ii/en/apost_exhortations/documents/hf_jp-ii
_exh_19811122_familiaris-consortio.html.

has written of the need to give young people "very spe-cial attention so that they may learn the true meaning of love and prepare for it with an appropriate education in sexuality, without letting themselves be distracted by ephemeral messages that prevent them from reaching the essence of the truth at stake."[24]

Conversations need to go far beyond biology. Put everything in the context of God's love for us. Before puberty—before 12 years of age or earlier—give your son or daughter a clear understanding of the realities and the beauty of human love and an explanation of why pornog-raphy, masturbation, and occasions of sin are so damag-ing. Talk about purity, self-understanding, and the role of emotions. Don't leave it to one talk, but have ongoing conversations. Ensure your son or daughter are comfort-able talking and asking questions. Keep the line open. Later, share rich conversations about social life, about courtship, about your own experiences, about God's plan for our happiness. And talk about the strength and sup-port you draw from the sacrament of matrimony.

24. Benedict XVI, Angelus (October 5, 2008). Vatican website: https://www.vatican.va/content/benedict-xvi/en/angelus/2008/documents/hf_ben-xvi_ang_20081005.html.

Marriage
Model these convictions, attitudes, and actions, and talk about them to your child: • Holy Purity • Temperance • Integrity
Ages for principal focus on these goals: ten years and upwards
Pray about these areas of example in your own life as a parent. • Am I grateful every day for this great sacrament by which two persons live completely for each other? Do I understand that caring for my spouse is my highway to heaven? • From the love of their parents, children understand what God's love must be like: unconditional, encouraging, self-sacrificing, affectionate. Do I convey this love as authentically as possible? • Do I have trust in God, that the great graces of the sacrament of marriage will bring us to holiness if we rely on them? • Do I strive to be united with my spouse, never arguing in front of the children, being the first to apologize after any disagreement, and being reconciled on the same day? • In our relationship do I acknowledge my faults, or am I the type of person who looks to blame? • Do I love my spouse with his or her defects, understanding that there are no ideal marriages but that God uses the differences between us to bring us to holiness?

- Do I love my spouse as he or she wishes to be loved? Or do I make the mistake of loving them on my own terms?
- Do I talk about the beauty of holy purity? Do I have deep personal conversations with each my children from the age of ten or so upwards, talking about God's great gifts of sex and love?

Education of head: Sow these convictions in your child.

- In life we are called to live for others.
- Holy purity is the great virtue whereby we put nothing in our lives above love of God. Let us ask each day that God grant us this virtue in abundance.
- The values of our family sometimes contrast with the negative values of society. These other values may be attractive, but at their heart they neither please God nor lead to happiness.

Education of heart: Education of a child's desires and feelings.

- How good God is for giving us a family where we learn about him and about the happiness we receive in serving others.
- We desire to support each other constantly with our prayers.
- We fill our family life with happiness and service.
- We try to please each other.
- We trust each other. I show my love by my trust.

CHAPTER 9

Final Thoughts

It is precisely in the family—a communion of persons among whom reigns a free disinterested and generous love—one leans to love. The family is a true school of love.

—Blessed Álvaro del Portillo[1]

Every family by nature is a sheltered environment, but protection is not the same as circling the wagons. By sheltering children we are buying time to train

---

1. Álvaro del Portillo, "A very large family," *Mundo Cristiano*, issue no. 385, 1994, p. 26.

and educate them to think clearly and to love God with all their hearts, souls, minds, and strength. Let every lesson in our home be of love of God and others. Let us each strive to create "a domestic church and a leaven of new life for society," as Pope Francis has written.[2]

In this way too we create homes that are beacons for other families. David Lejeune, a marketing guru and marriage educator, insists, "Let them in! Let others see the beauty of authentic Christian families."[3] Let us never forget that we are called by St. Paul to "Shine on the world like bright stars. You are offering it the word of life."

By doing this we are raising our children to be so happy in this life, and to be dizzily joyful in eternity. And in this we too discover our vocation to holiness.

In conclusion, I have three thoughts for you.

#1 Good habits also apply to adults.

We all need to work the spectrum of virtues into our own characters. Our happiness and holiness depend on it, but, for

---

2. *Amoris Laetitia*, 292.
3. Personal anecdote of David Lejeune, Address to the Renaissance of Marriage Conference, Sydney, Australia, October 21-22, 2016.

a parent, there is the added incentive that example is almost everything. Otherwise children will not be life-ready.

It is so easy to lose our rectitude of intention and act selfishly. Bryan, a wonderful teacher on the staff of my last school, told me this story:

> I was rushing my two-year-old to get ready for bed. I was not giving him my full affection, and certainly not my full attention, and he was resisting. Suddenly I realized, "I'm making him go at my pace. I'm doing this too much for my *own* reasons." I changed my approach. I went at his pace, and he settled right down. I won't forget that lesson.

The development of our own character is the first prerequisite for effective parenting. Remember there are four key strengths:

1. Train our impulsive desires so they do not lead us to offend God or others.
2. Focus our attention on Jesus himself, our model, and let us build habits of daily prayer and sacraments. Our children will love what we love.
3. Give ourselves to others and help them to pursue their goals, not ours.

4. Set goals for ourselves and listen to the feedback of our better half and our children.

#2 Those who face with faith even the most taxing challenges tend to weather them better.

Running a school brings an awareness of the great difficulties so many families face. One day I received a phone call from Colombia, from a family intending to emigrate to Australia the next year and enroll their boys. I sent Pilar Vargas, the mother, information and put things in motion. Some months later she rang again to say the move was on hold because her brother, Miguel, had just been kidnapped by the rebel group FARC. I told her we would pray for his safety. When the family did arrive, she and her husband, Gabriel, told me the story. All through the three months of his captivity, while Miguel had been held in appalling conditions, the family, at the urging of Pilar's father, were praying to then-Blessed Josemaría for his safety and release. It turned out that the crucial information for the rescue of Miguel was obtained on the feast day of Blessed Josemaría.

The story gets better, but first it gets worse.

After the family arrived in Sydney, the nightmare returned. Pilar's sister, Luisa, a young mother of five, was then kidnapped. Again, the grandfather urged everyone to pray. The first months passed with practically no information from the kidnappers—all part of their psychological strategy. A full year passed. On the news were stories of kidnapped persons who had been killed, and others who were taken years before and were still in the jungle. The grandfather kept everyone praying. Finally the breakthrough came. Luisa was released on the date that the canonization of Blessed Josemaría was announced.

On her release, Luisa wrote a most beautiful letter to the parents, staff, and students of her nephews' and nieces' schools. She wrote stoically of the trials of jungle life, compassionately of her young kidnappers, and most of all she wrote of the awakening of a great trust in God:

> These seventeen months have taught me the importance of being a really good friend of God— an unconditional friend—and that in all the joys, sadness, difficulties, and successes we might experience in this life, our Lord is there to show us how to accept them with love, joy, and generosity. . . . I

have been given another chance to become a better person.

Luisa realized that the very challenges she faced with God's help gave her a second chance to be holy. When we face difficulties with prayer, not only will we cope, but most importantly we will bring to fruition the very purpose of our life. We will become holy.

#3 Never give up on God.

The most famous instance of persistent prayer is the conversion of St. Augustine. For a decade or more his mother Monica prayed, fasted, and encouraged him. These persevering and heartfelt prayers brought her son out of a long term extramarital relationship and out of a second affair, then back to his faith, to the priesthood, and later to prominence as one of the greatest theologians and doctors of the Church. Her prayers brought the mother of Augustine's child to the Catholic faith as well, and Monica to holiness.

If I employ someone, it is my duty to give that person all the help and training they need to work well. Yet God is better than the best employer. God knows what he is asking of us, and he always gives us the assistance to do it properly. Sit with God every day and talk about what each child needs and how you can provide this. To raise your children well is your most important business, and what manager does not focus on the daily needs of the business? Above all, a good manager works at eye level, they are close to their workers, and they inculcate ownership and personal responsibility at every level. In the same way, the best parents teach their children to love God and others despite the milk and honey. This is the core business of parenting.